1913 Larkin's Labour War

BAINTE DEN STOC

WITHDRAWN FROM
DÚN LAOGHAIRE-RATHDOWN COUNTY
LIBRARY STOCK

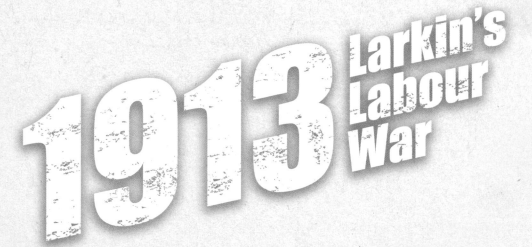

1913 Larkin's Labour War

WRITTEN & DRAWN BY

GERRY HUNT

COLOURED BY

ALAN NOLAN

THE O'BRIEN PRESS
DUBLIN

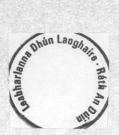

First published 2013 by The O'Brien Press Limited
12 Terenure Road East, Rathgar, Dublin 6, Ireland
Tel: +353 1 4923333; Fax: +353 1 4292777
Email: books@obrien.ie
Website: www.obrien.ie

ISBN: 978-1-84717-583-0

1 2 3 4 5 6 7 8 9
13 14 15 16

Printed and bound in Poland by Białostockie Zakłady Graficzne S.A.
The paper in this book is produced using pulp from managed forests

The O'Brien Press receives assistance from

the arts council
an chomhairle ealaíon
funding literature
artscouncil.ie

For all the volunteers in the St Vincent De Paul who work tirelessly in these
awful times foisted on us by the untouchables up there
G.H.

For Dad
A.N.

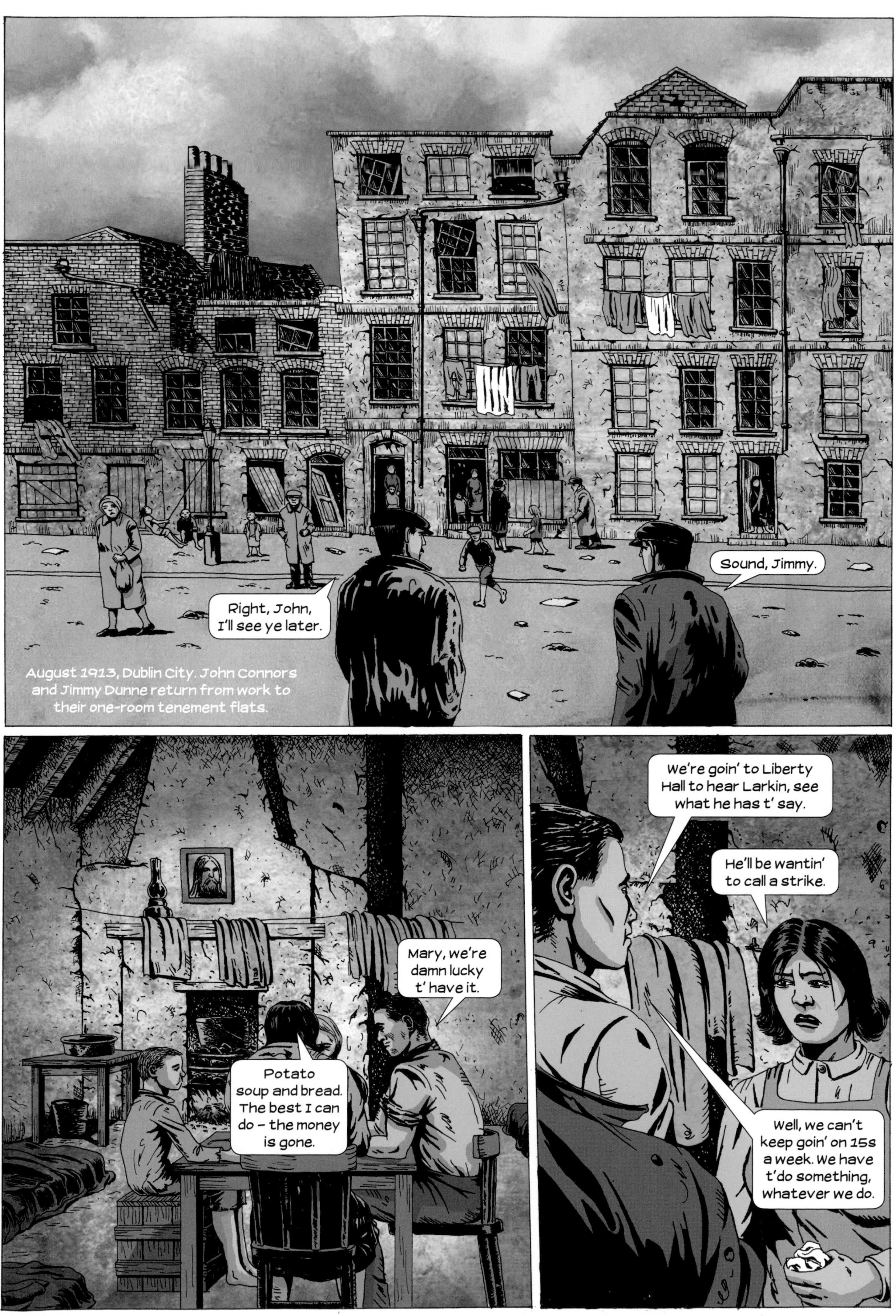
August 1913, Dublin City. John Connors and Jimmy Dunne return from work to their one-room tenement flats.
Right, John, I'll see ye later.
Sound, Jimmy.
Potato soup and bread. The best I can do – the money is gone.
Mary, we're damn lucky t' have it.
We're goin' to Liberty Hall to hear Larkin, see what he has t' say.
He'll be wantin' to call a strike.
Well, we can't keep goin' on 15s a week. We have t'do something, whatever we do.

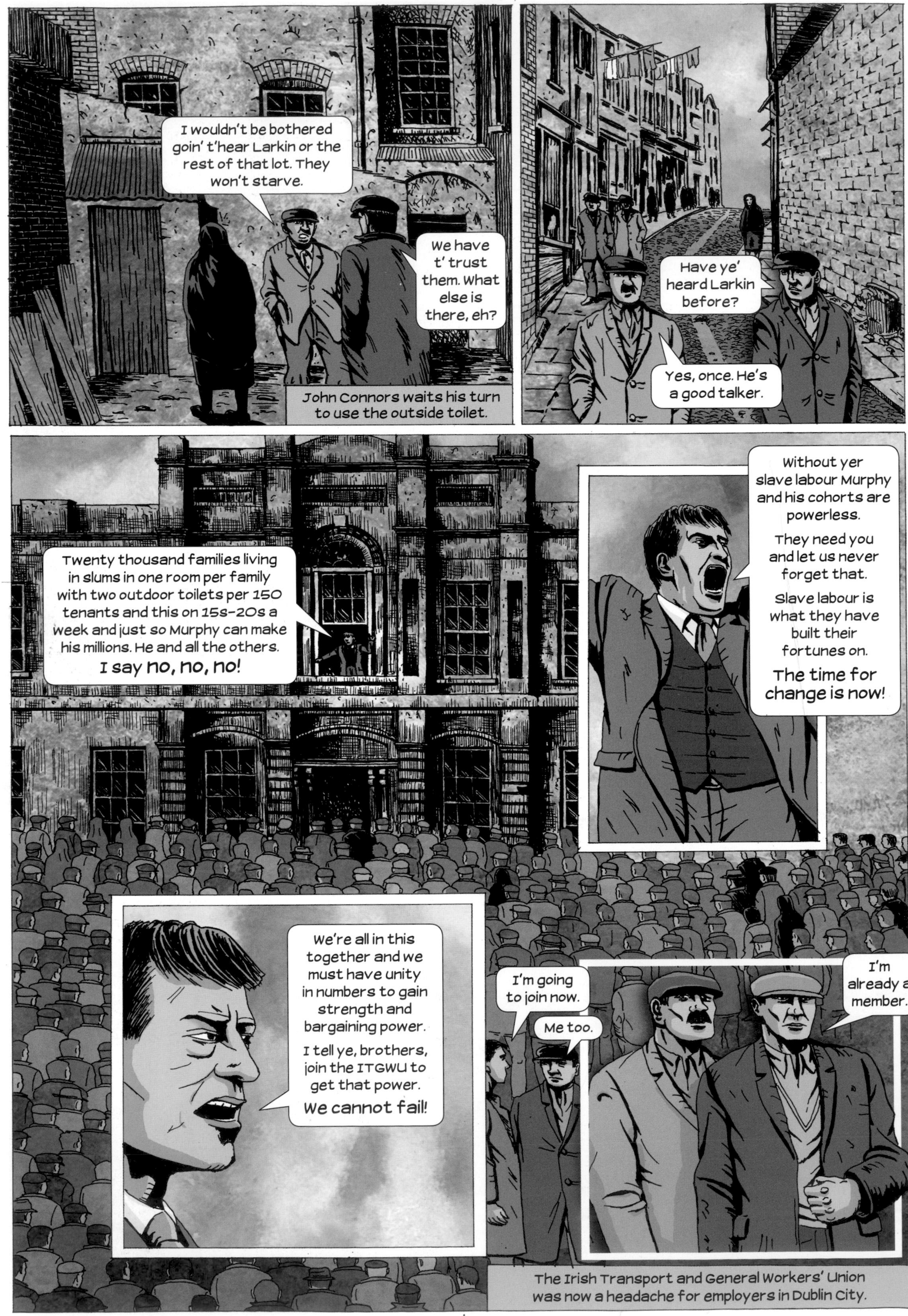
I wouldn't be bothered goin' t'hear Larkin or the rest of that lot. They won't starve.
We have t' trust them. What else is there, eh?
John Connors waits his turn to use the outside toilet.
Have ye' heard Larkin before?
Yes, once. He's a good talker.
Twenty thousand families living in slums in one room per family with two outdoor toilets per 150 tenants and this on 15s–20s a week and just so Murphy can make his millions. He and all the others. I say no, no, no!
Without yer slave labour Murphy and his cohorts are powerless. They need you and let us never forget that. Slave labour is what they have built their fortunes on. The time for change is now!
We're all in this together and we must have unity in numbers to gain strength and bargaining power. I tell ye, brothers, join the ITGWU to get that power. We cannot fail!
I'm going to join now.
Me too.
I'm already a member.
The Irish Transport and General Workers' Union was now a headache for employers in Dublin City.

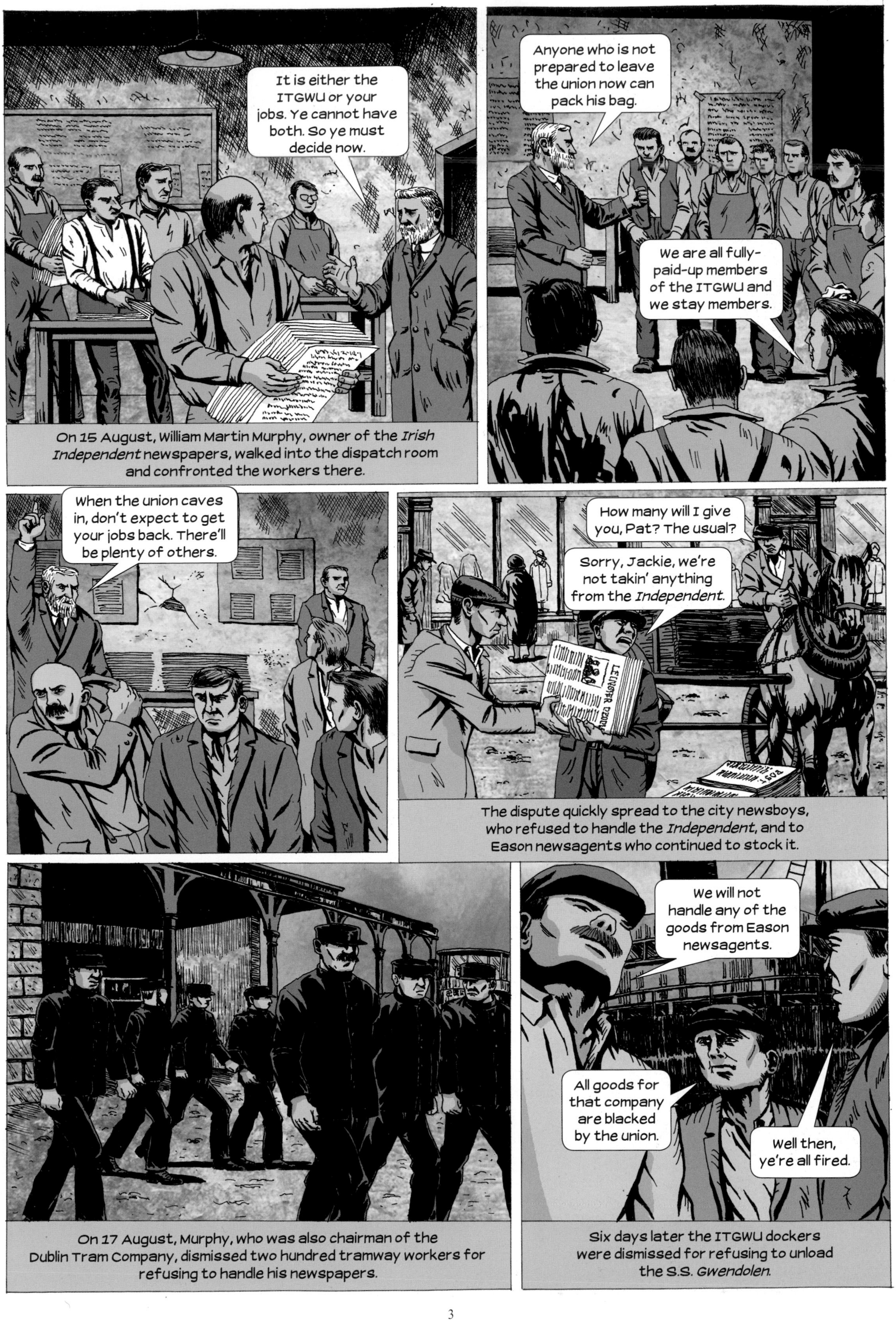
It is either the ITGWU or your jobs. Ye cannot have both. So ye must decide now.
On 15 August, William Martin Murphy, owner of the *Irish Independent* newspapers, walked into the dispatch room and confronted the workers there.
Anyone who is not prepared to leave the union now can pack his bag.
We are all fully-paid-up members of the ITGWU and we stay members.
When the union caves in, don't expect to get your jobs back. There'll be plenty of others.
How many will I give you, Pat? The usual?
Sorry, Jackie, we're not takin' anything from the *Independent*.
The dispute quickly spread to the city newsboys, who refused to handle the *Independent*, and to Eason newsagents who continued to stock it.
On 17 August, Murphy, who was also chairman of the Dublin Tram Company, dismissed two hundred tramway workers for refusing to handle his newspapers.
We will not handle any of the goods from Eason newsagents.
All goods for that company are blacked by the union.
Well then, ye're all fired.
Six days later the ITGWU dockers were dismissed for refusing to unload the S.S. *Gwendolen*.

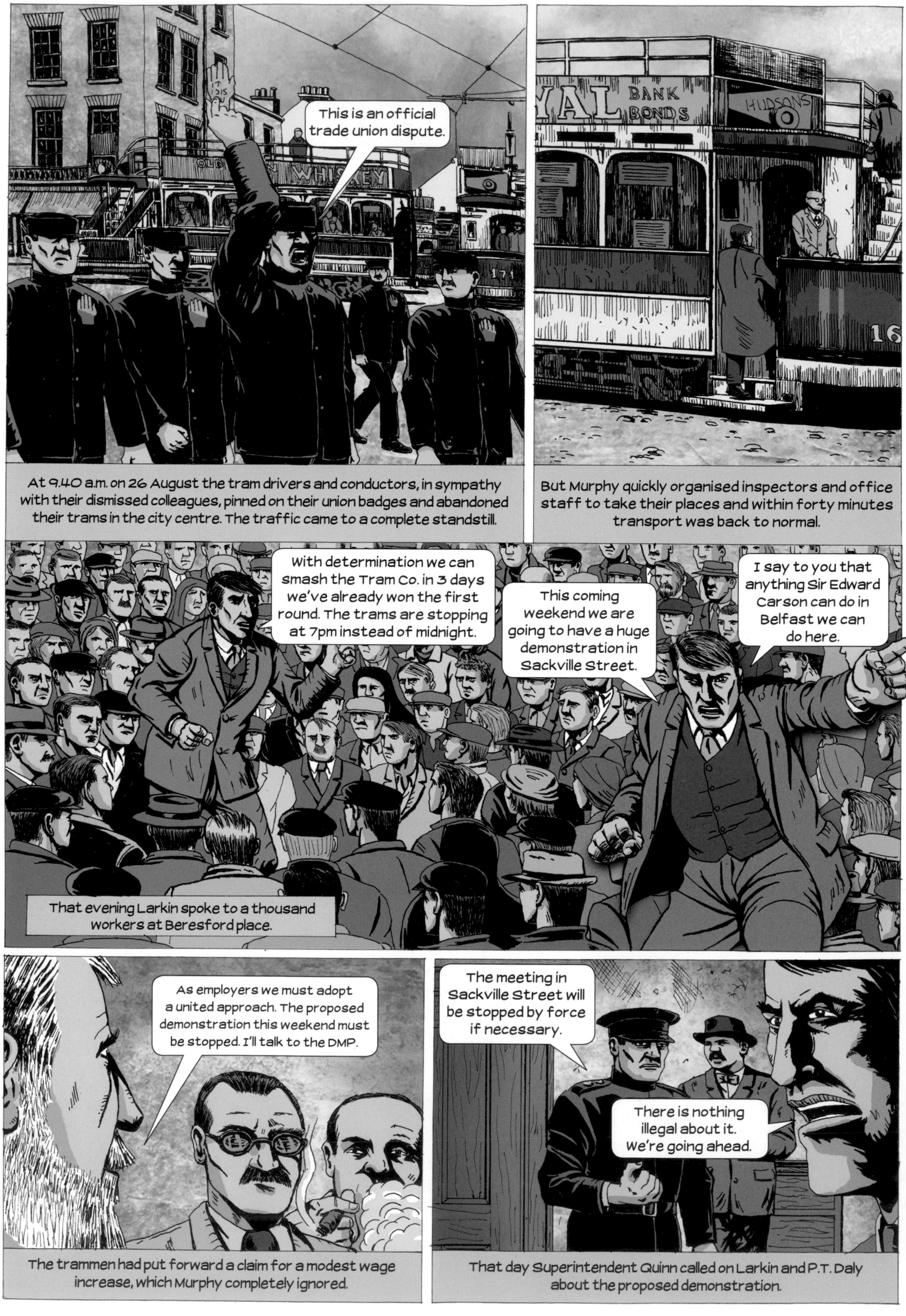

This is an official trade union dispute.
At 9.40 a.m. on 26 August the tram drivers and conductors, in sympathy with their dismissed colleagues, pinned on their union badges and abandoned their trams in the city centre. The traffic came to a complete standstill.
BANK BONDS
But Murphy quickly organised inspectors and office staff to take their places and within forty minutes transport was back to normal.
With determination we can smash the Tram Co. in 3 days we've already won the first round. The trams are stopping at 7pm instead of midnight.
This coming weekend we are going to have a huge demonstration in Sackville Street.
I say to you that anything Sir Edward Carson can do in Belfast we can do here.
That evening Larkin spoke to a thousand workers at Beresford place.
As employers we must adopt a united approach. The proposed demonstration this weekend must be stopped. I'll talk to the DMP.
The trammen had put forward a claim for a modest wage increase, which Murphy completely ignored.
The meeting in Sackville Street will be stopped by force if necessary.
There is nothing illegal about it. We're going ahead.
That day Superintendent Quinn called on Larkin and P.T. Daly about the proposed demonstration.

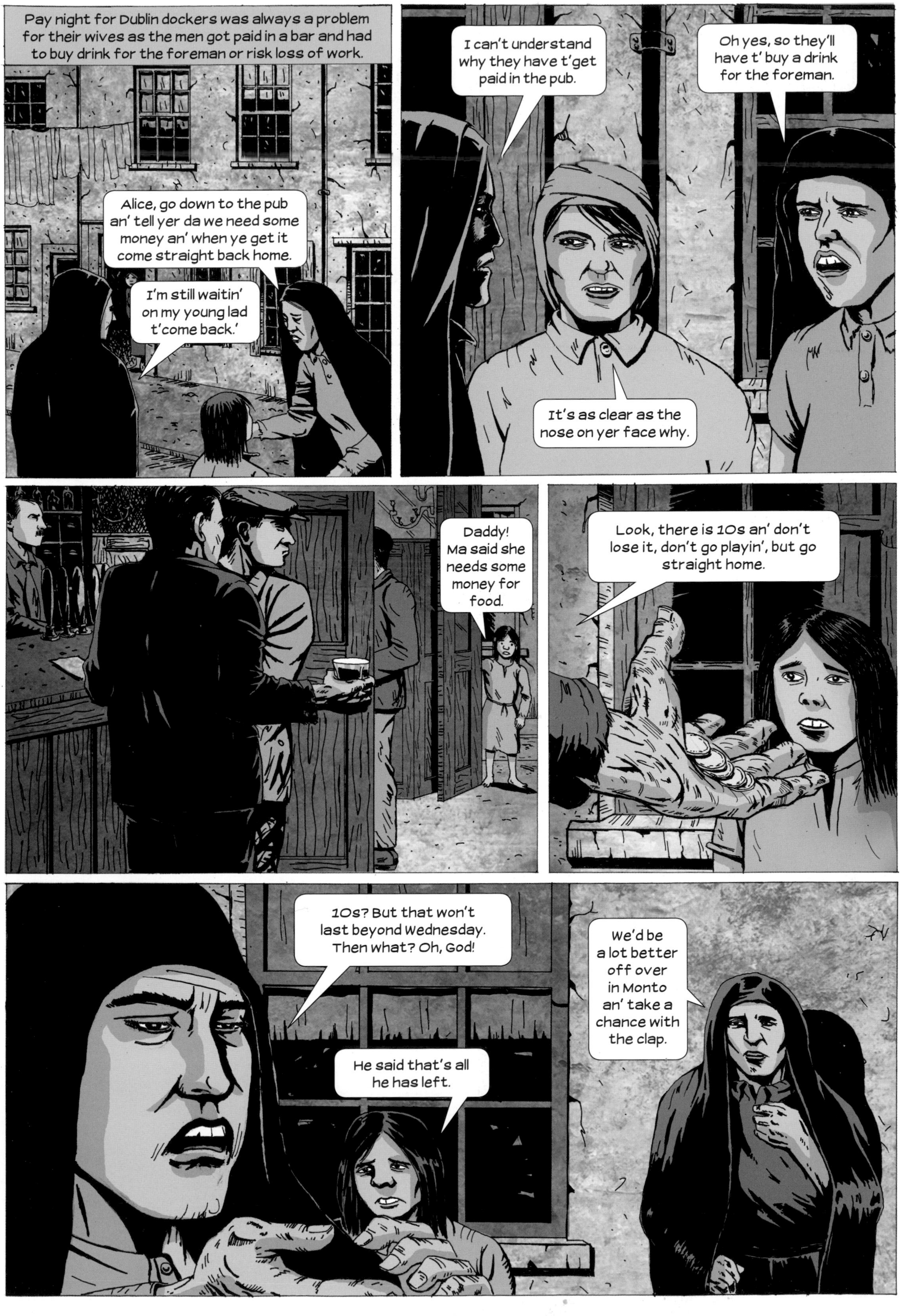
Pay night for Dublin dockers was always a problem for their wives as the men got paid in a bar and had to buy drink for the foreman or risk loss of work.
Alice, go down to the pub an' tell yer da we need some money an' when ye get it come straight back home.
I'm still waitin' on my young lad t'come back.'
I can't understand why they have t'get paid in the pub.
Oh yes, so they'll have t' buy a drink for the foreman.
It's as clear as the nose on yer face why.
Daddy! Ma said she needs some money for food.
Look, there is 10s an' don't lose it, don't go playin', but go straight home.
10s? But that won't last beyond Wednesday. Then what? Oh, God!
He said that's all he has left.
We'd be a lot better off over in Monto an' take a chance with the clap.

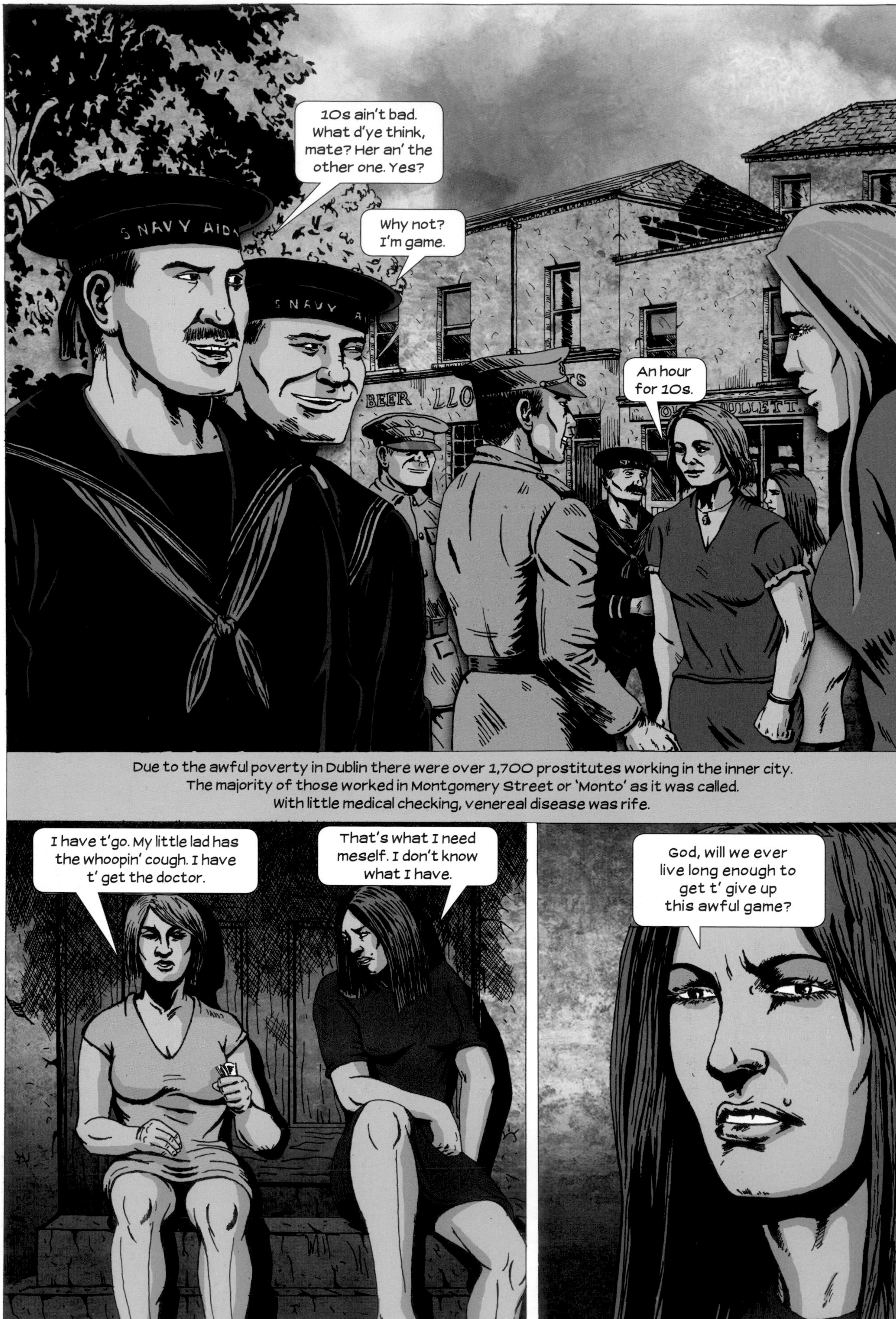
10s ain't bad. What d'ye think, mate? Her an' the other one. Yes?
Why not? I'm game.
BEER
An hour for 10s.
Due to the awful poverty in Dublin there were over 1,700 prostitutes working in the inner city. The majority of those worked in Montgomery Street or 'Monto' as it was called. With little medical checking, venereal disease was rife.
I have t'go. My little lad has the whoopin' cough. I have t' get the doctor.
That's what I need meself. I don't know what I have.
God, will we ever live long enough to get t' give up this awful game?

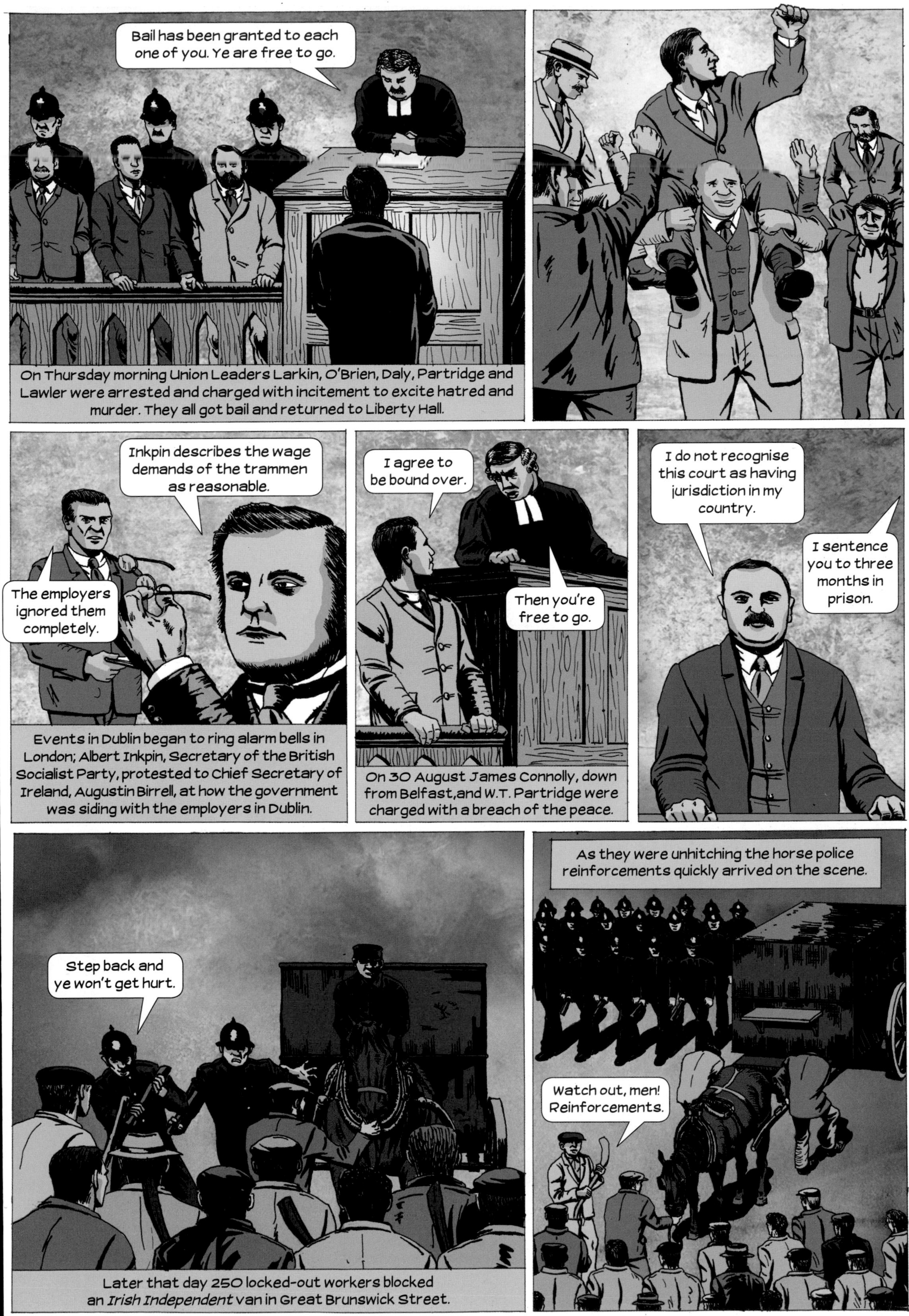
Bail has been granted to each one of you. Ye are free to go.
On Thursday morning Union Leaders Larkin, O'Brien, Daly, Partridge and Lawler were arrested and charged with incitement to excite hatred and murder. They all got bail and returned to Liberty Hall.
Inkpin describes the wage demands of the trammen as reasonable.
The employers ignored them completely.
Events in Dublin began to ring alarm bells in London; Albert Inkpin, Secretary of the British Socialist Party, protested to Chief Secretary of Ireland, Augustin Birrell, at how the government was siding with the employers in Dublin.
I agree to be bound over.
Then you're free to go.
On 30 August James Connolly, down from Belfast, and W.T. Partridge were charged with a breach of the peace.
I do not recognise this court as having jurisdiction in my country.
I sentence you to three months in prison.
Step back and ye won't get hurt.
Later that day 250 locked-out workers blocked an *Irish Independent* van in Great Brunswick Street.
As they were unhitching the horse police reinforcements quickly arrived on the scene.
Watch out, men! Reinforcements.

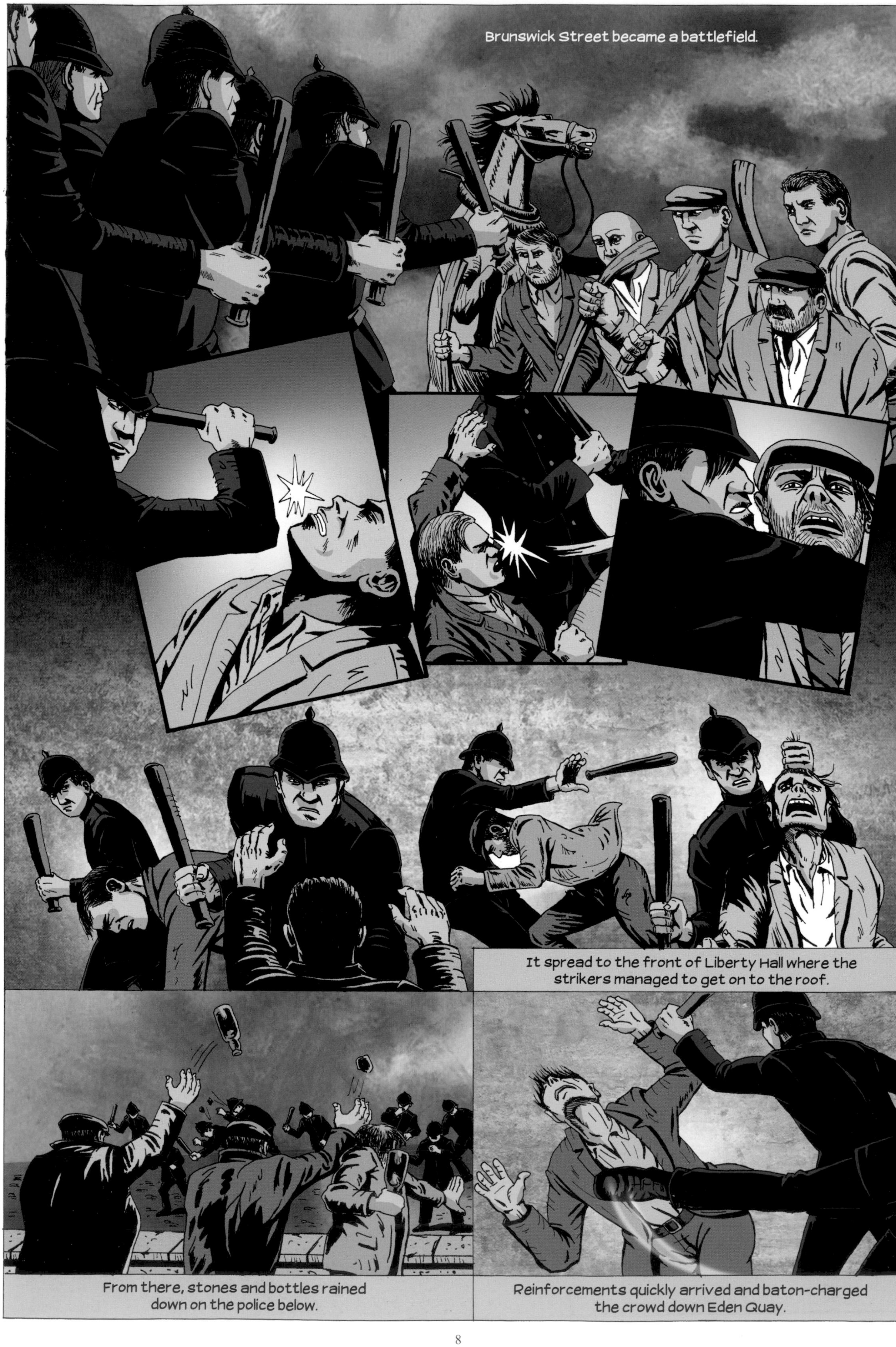
Brunswick Street became a battlefield.
It spread to the front of Liberty Hall where the strikers managed to get on to the roof.
From there, stones and bottles rained down on the police below.
Reinforcements quickly arrived and baton-charged the crowd down Eden Quay.

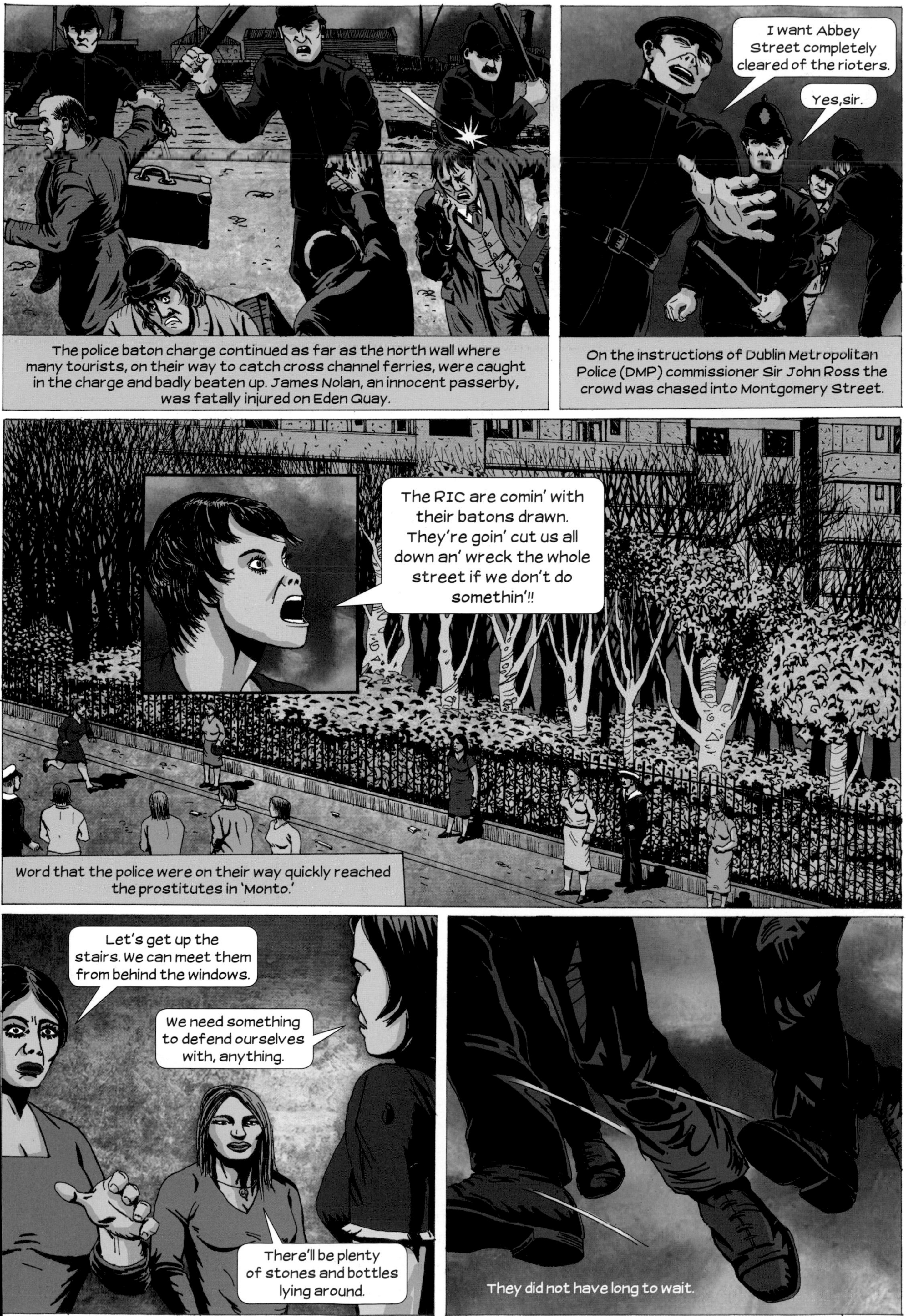

The police baton charge continued as far as the north wall where many tourists, on their way to catch cross channel ferries, were caught in the charge and badly beaten up. James Nolan, an innocent passerby, was fatally injured on Eden Quay.
I want Abbey Street completely cleared of the rioters.
Yes, sir.
On the instructions of Dublin Metropolitan Police (DMP) commissioner Sir John Ross the crowd was chased into Montgomery Street.
The RIC are comin' with their batons drawn. They're goin' cut us all down an' wreck the whole street if we don't do somethin'!!
Word that the police were on their way quickly reached the prostitutes in 'Monto.'
Let's get up the stairs. We can meet them from behind the windows.
We need something to defend ourselves with, anything.
There'll be plenty of stones and bottles lying around.
They did not have long to wait.

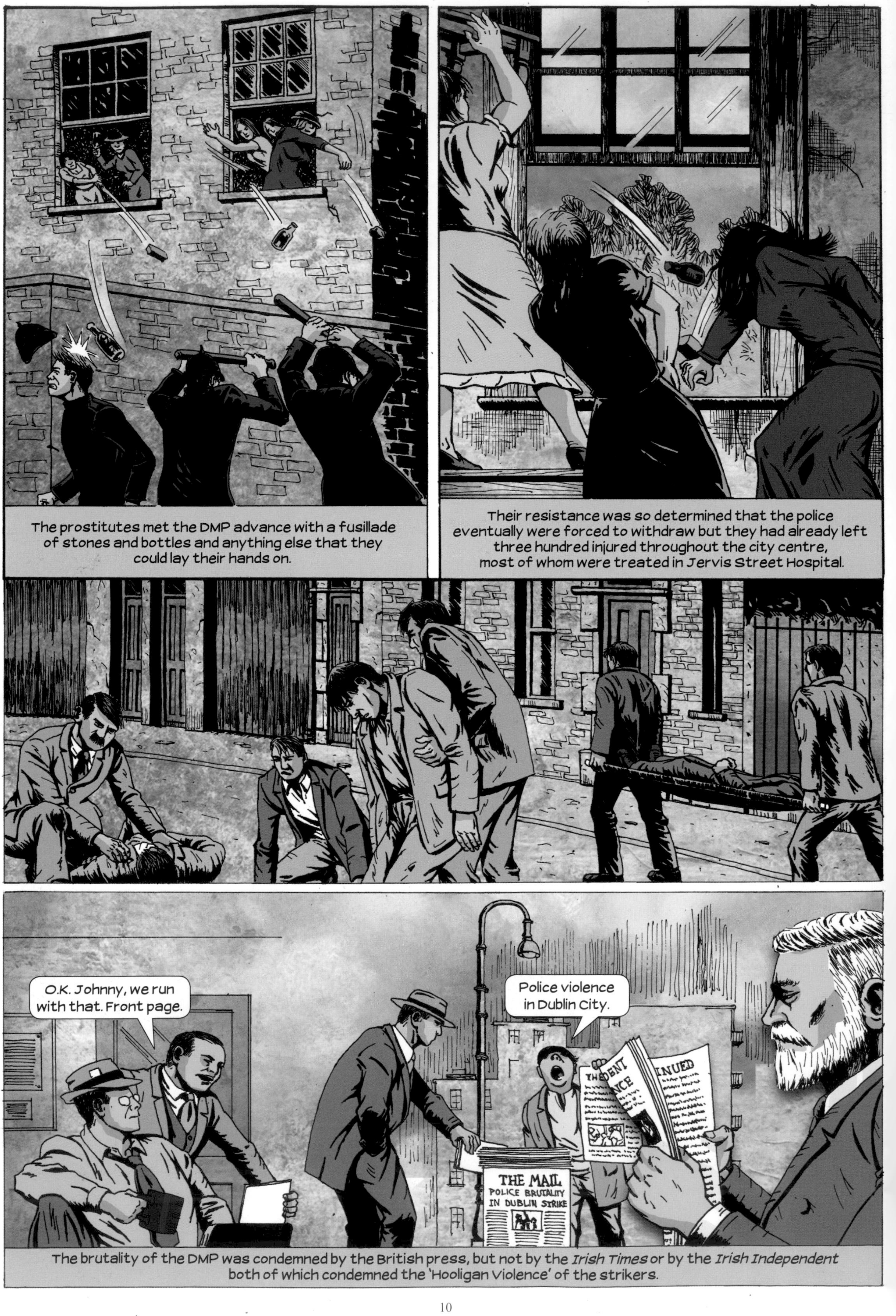
The prostitutes met the DMP advance with a fusillade of stones and bottles and anything else that they could lay their hands on.
Their resistance was so determined that the police eventually were forced to withdraw but they had already left three hundred injured throughout the city centre, most of whom were treated in Jervis Street Hospital.
O.K. Johnny, we run with that. Front page.
Police violence in Dublin City.
THE MAIL
POLICE BRUTALITY IN DUBLIN STRIKE
The brutality of the DMP was condemned by the British press, but not by the *Irish Times* or by the *Irish Independent* both of which condemned the 'Hooligan Violence' of the strikers.

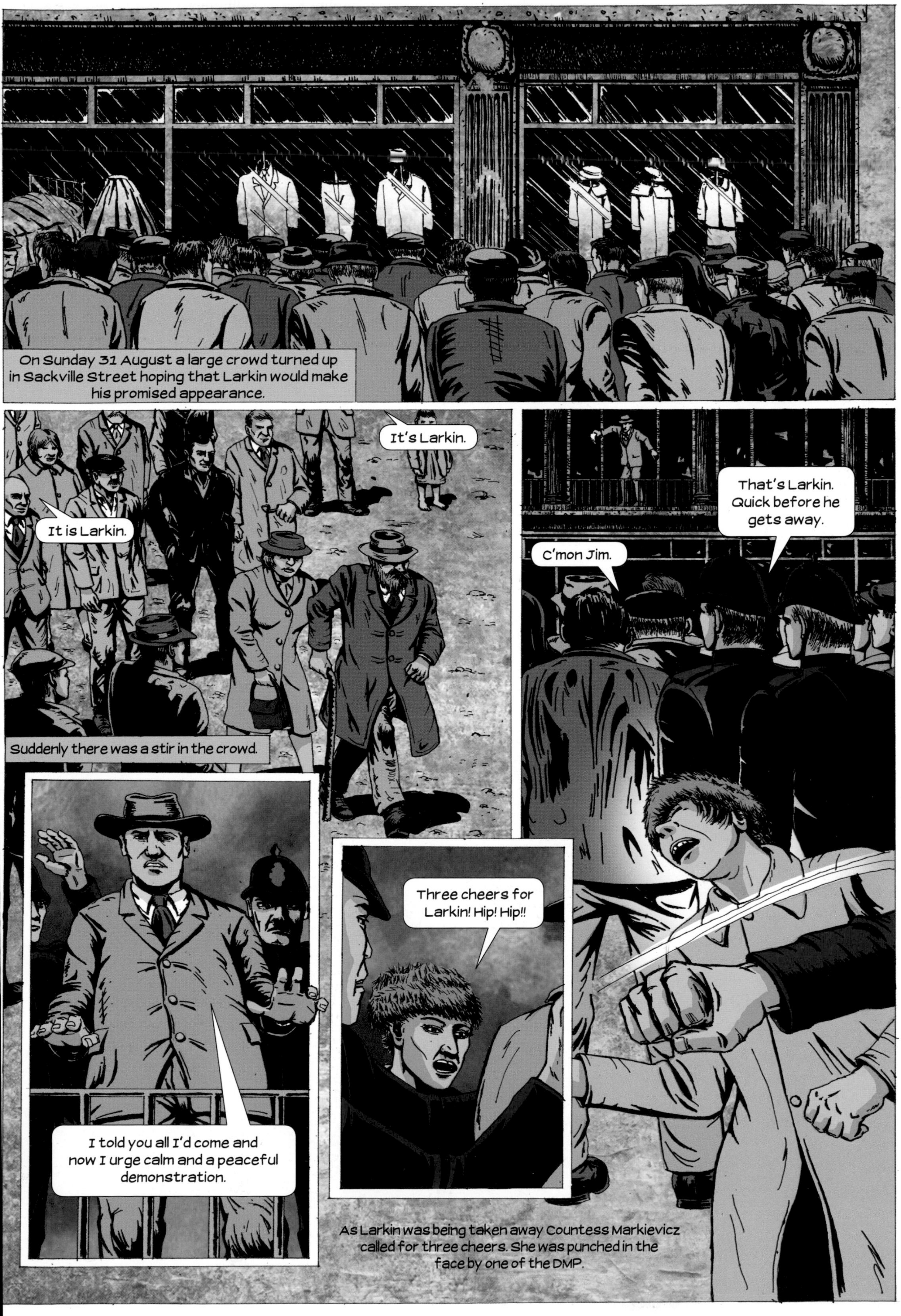

On Sunday 31 August a large crowd turned up in Sackville Street hoping that Larkin would make his promised appearance.
It's Larkin.
It is Larkin.
Suddenly there was a stir in the crowd.
That's Larkin. Quick before he gets away.
C'mon Jim.
I told you all I'd come and now I urge calm and a peaceful demonstration.
Three cheers for Larkin! Hip! Hip!!
As Larkin was being taken away Countess Markievicz called for three cheers. She was punched in the face by one of the DMP.

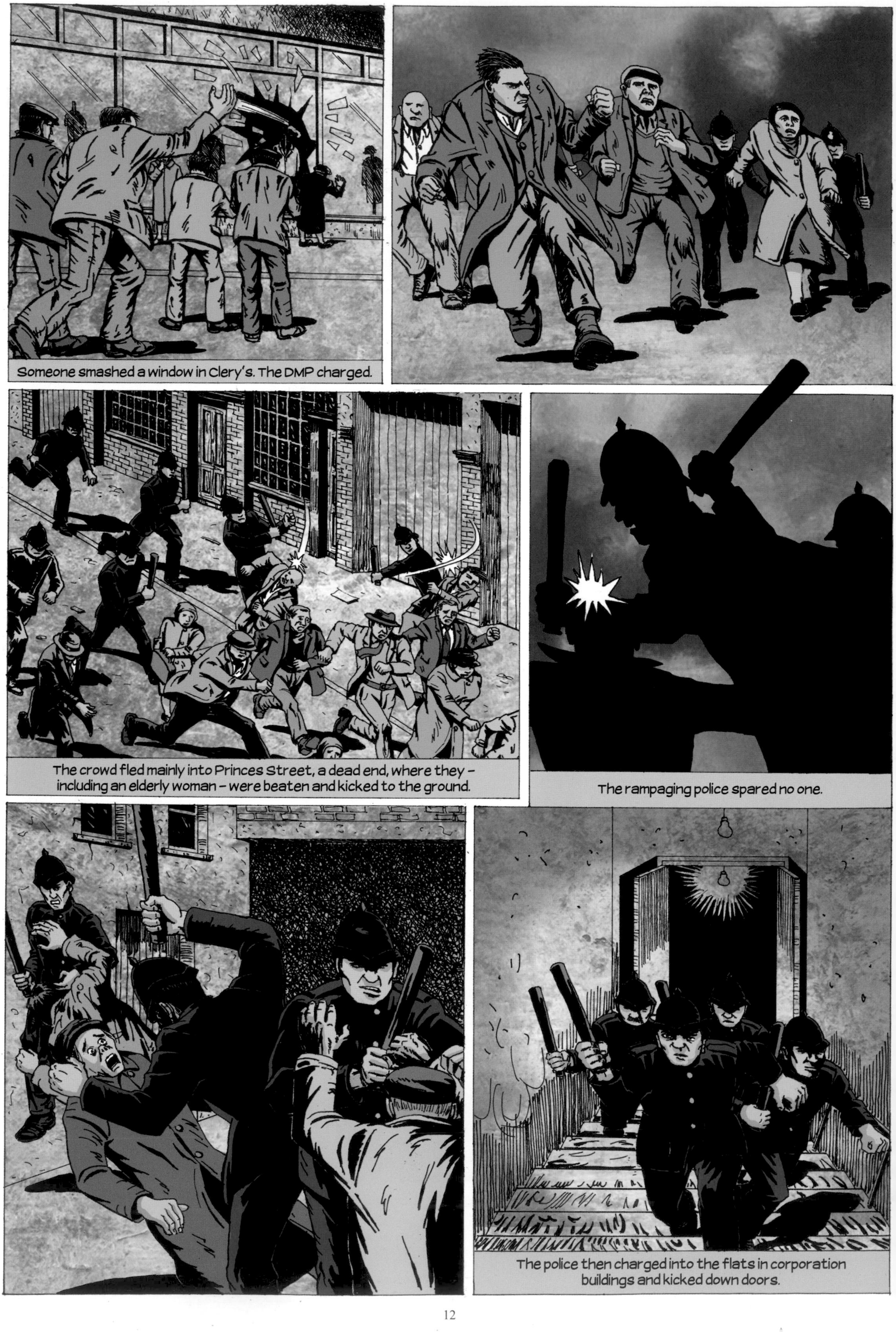
Someone smashed a window in Clery's. The DMP charged.
The crowd fled mainly into Princes Street, a dead end, where they – including an elderly woman – were beaten and kicked to the ground.
The rampaging police spared no one.
The police then charged into the flats in corporation buildings and kicked down doors.

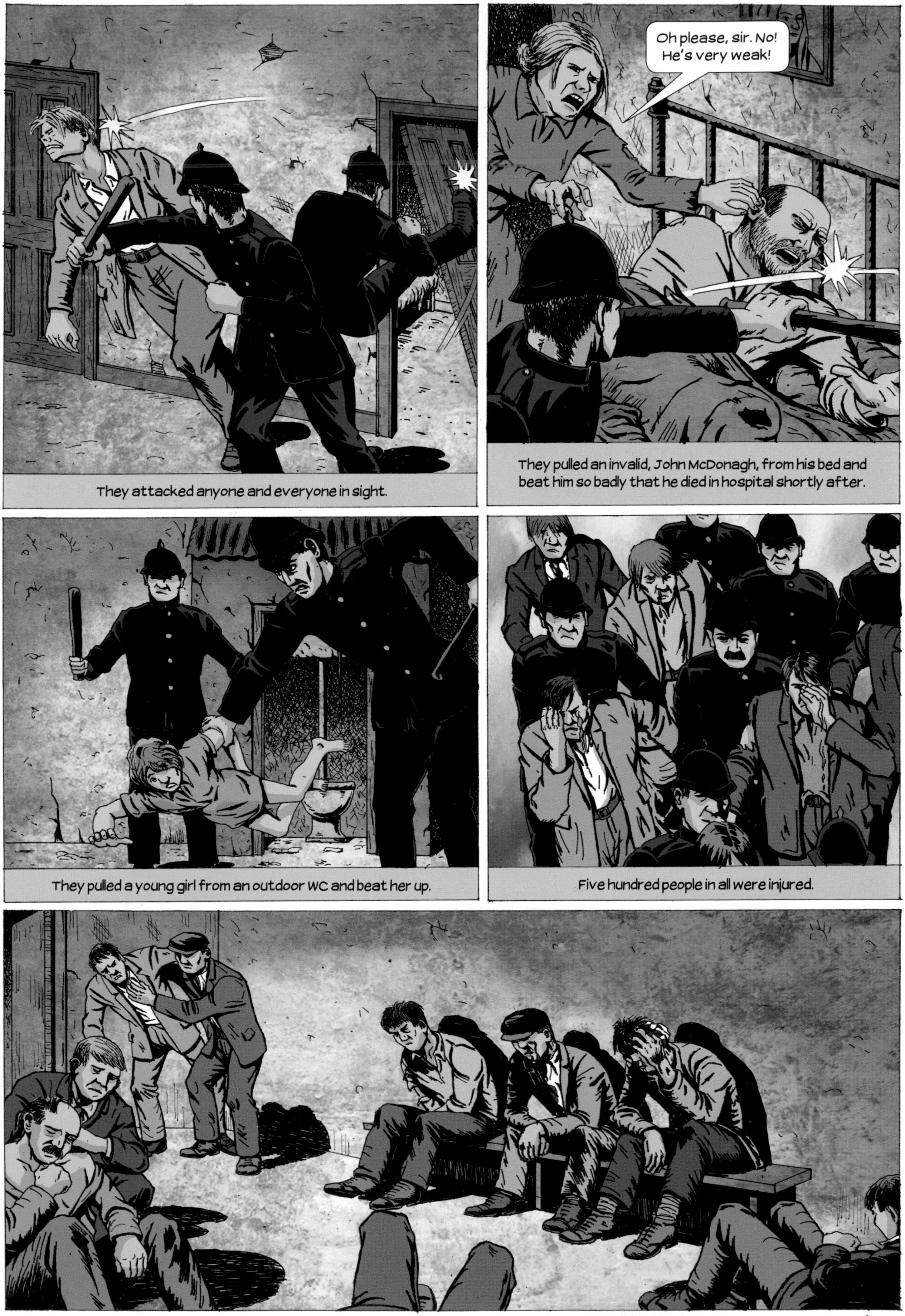
They attacked anyone and everyone in sight.
Oh please, sir. No! He's very weak!
They pulled an invalid, John McDonagh, from his bed and beat him so badly that he died in hospital shortly after.
They pulled a young girl from an outdoor WC and beat her up.
Five hundred people in all were injured.

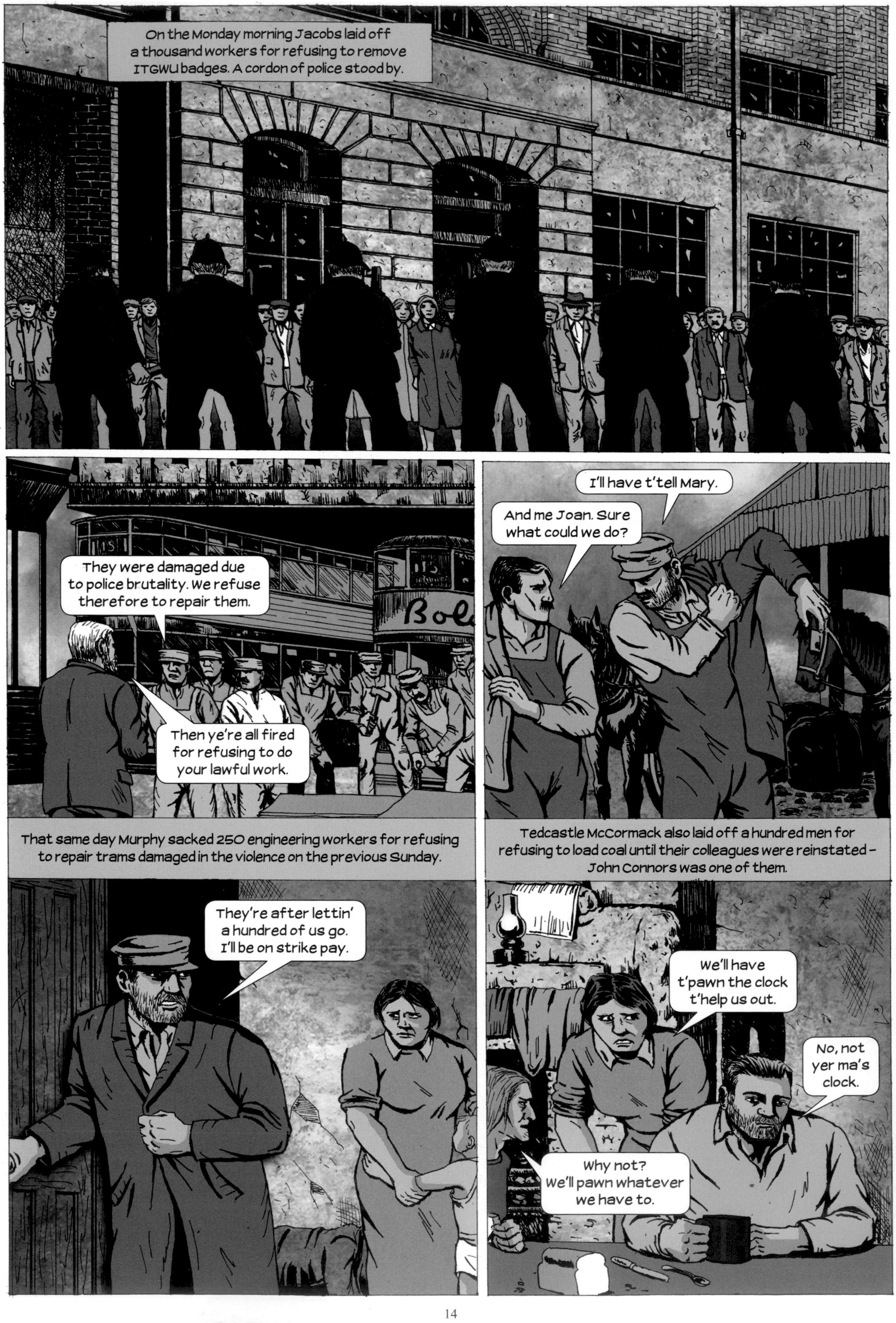
On the Monday morning Jacobs laid off a thousand workers for refusing to remove ITGWU badges. A cordon of police stood by.
They were damaged due to police brutality. We refuse therefore to repair them.
Then ye're all fired for refusing to do your lawful work.
That same day Murphy sacked 250 engineering workers for refusing to repair trams damaged in the violence on the previous Sunday.
I'll have t'tell Mary.
And me Joan. Sure what could we do?
Tedcastle McCormack also laid off a hundred men for refusing to load coal until their colleagues were reinstated – John Connors was one of them.
They're after lettin' a hundred of us go. I'll be on strike pay.
We'll have t'pawn the clock t'help us out.
No, not yer ma's clock.
Why not? We'll pawn whatever we have to.

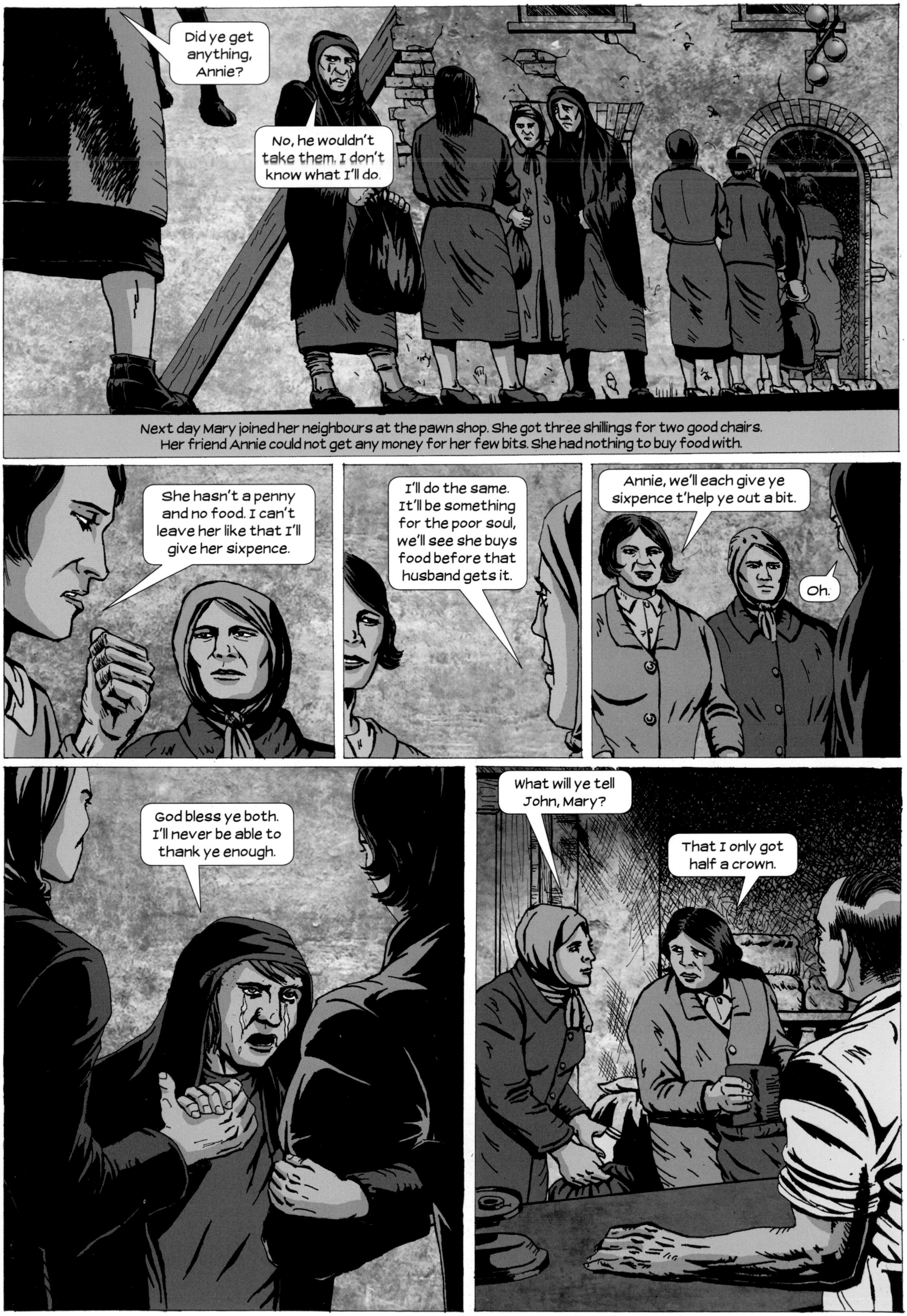
Did ye get anything, Annie?
No, he wouldn't take them. I don't know what I'll do.
Next day Mary joined her neighbours at the pawn shop. She got three shillings for two good chairs. Her friend Annie could not get any money for her few bits. She had nothing to buy food with.
She hasn't a penny and no food. I can't leave her like that I'll give her sixpence.
I'll do the same. It'll be something for the poor soul, we'll see she buys food before that husband gets it.
Annie, we'll each give ye sixpence t'help ye out a bit.
Oh.
God bless ye both. I'll never be able to thank ye enough.
What will ye tell John, Mary?
That I only got half a crown.

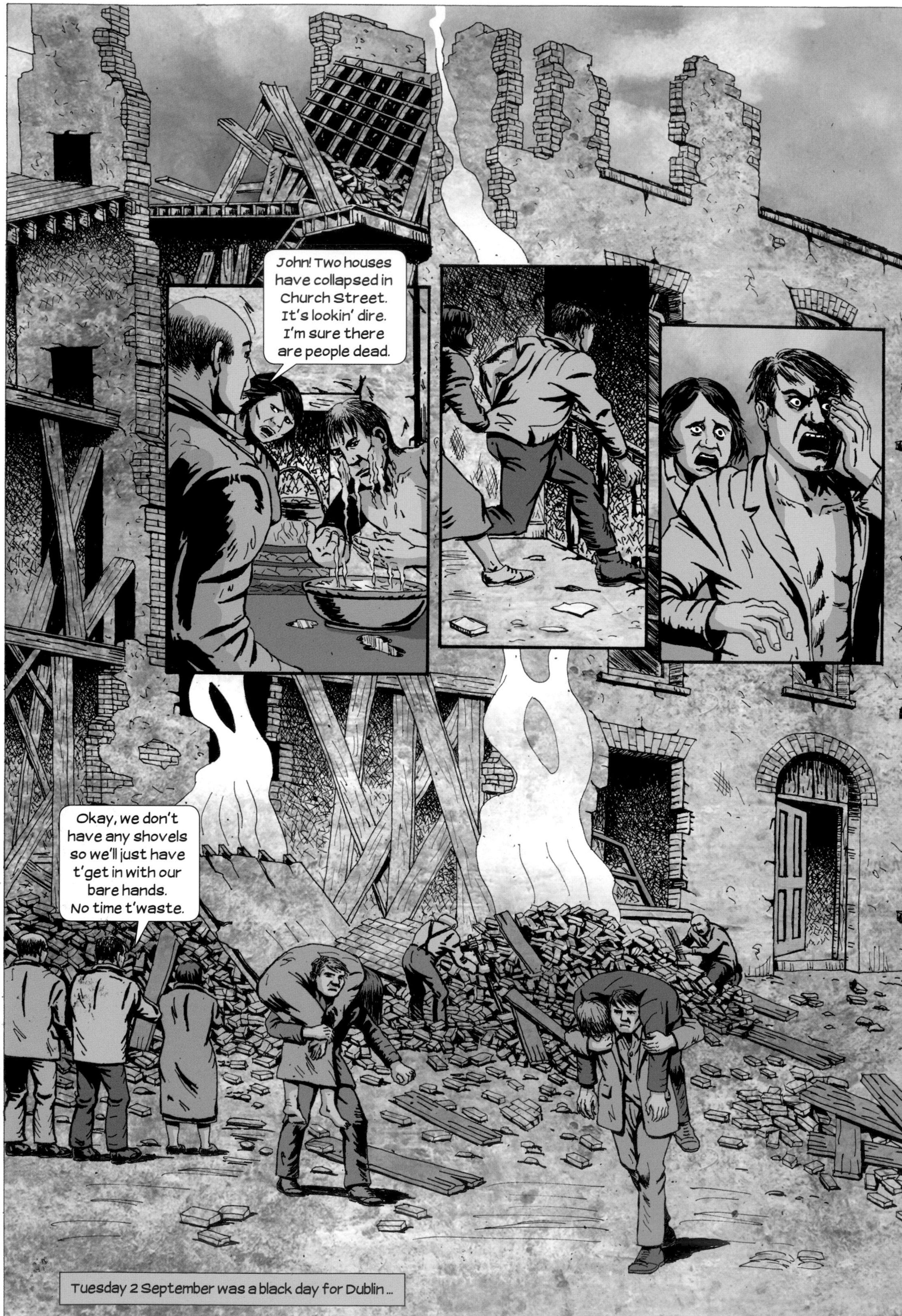
John! Two houses have collapsed in Church Street. It's lookin' dire. I'm sure there are people dead.
Okay, we don't have any shovels so we'll just have t'get in with our bare hands. No time t'waste.
Tuesday 2 September was a black day for Dublin ...

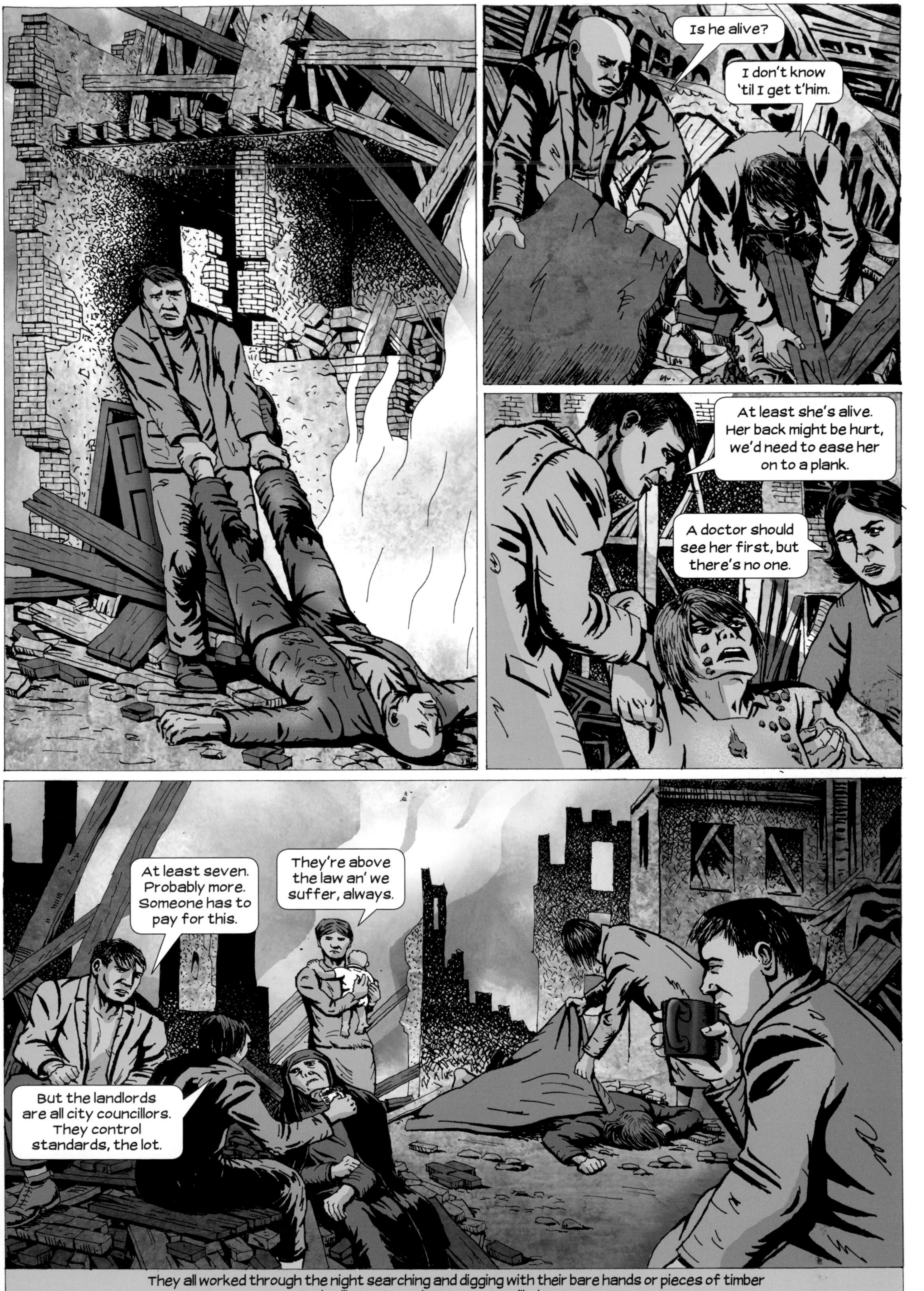
Is he alive?
I don't know 'til I get t'him.
At least she's alive. Her back might be hurt, we'd need to ease her on to a plank.
A doctor should see her first, but there's no one.
At least seven. Probably more. Someone has to pay for this.
They're above the law an' we suffer, always.
But the landlords are all city councillors. They control standards, the lot.
They all worked through the night searching and digging with their bare hands or pieces of timber and pulling out survivors or – more likely – corpses.

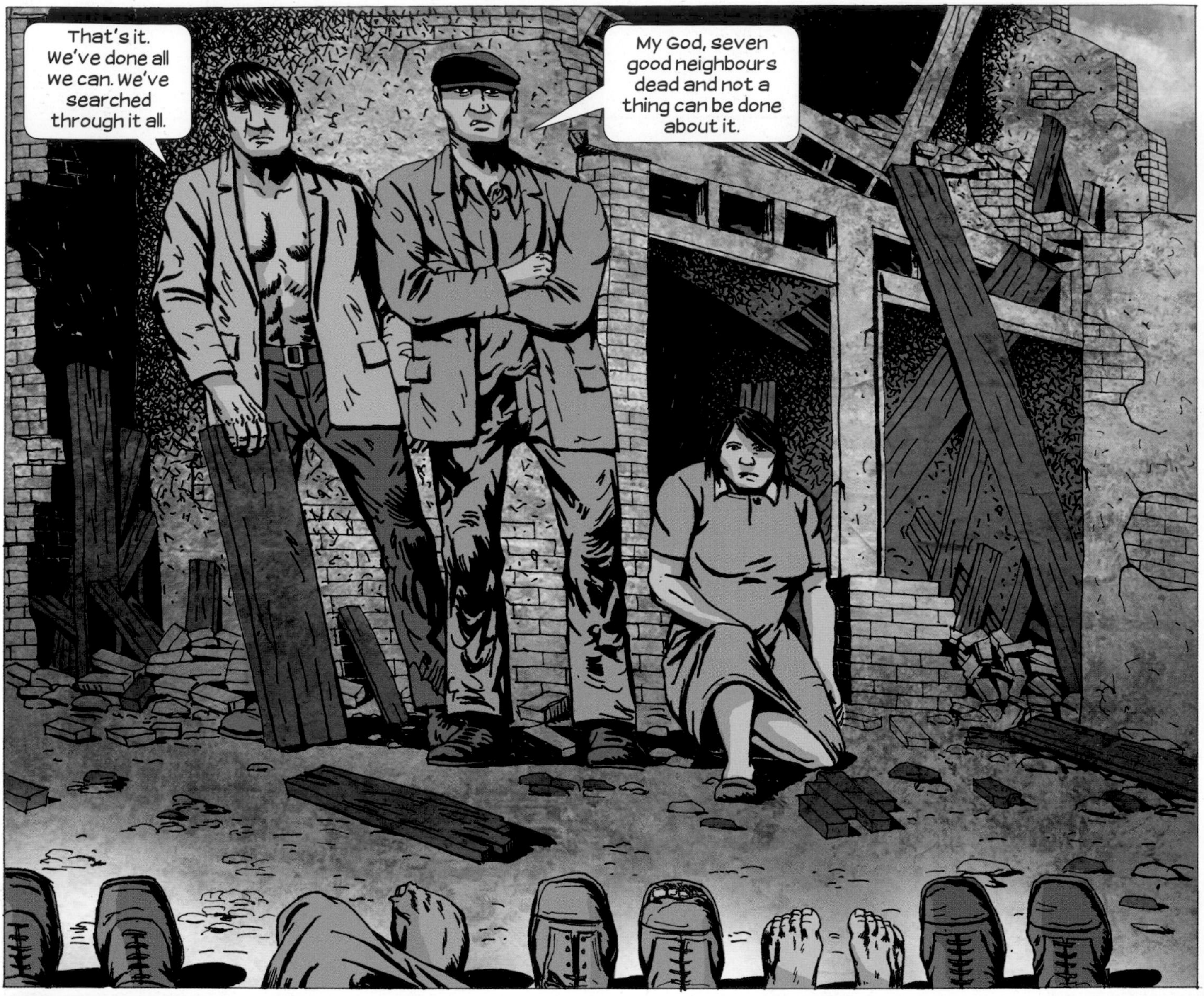
That's it. We've done all we can. We've searched through it all.
My God, seven good neighbours dead and not a thing can be done about it.

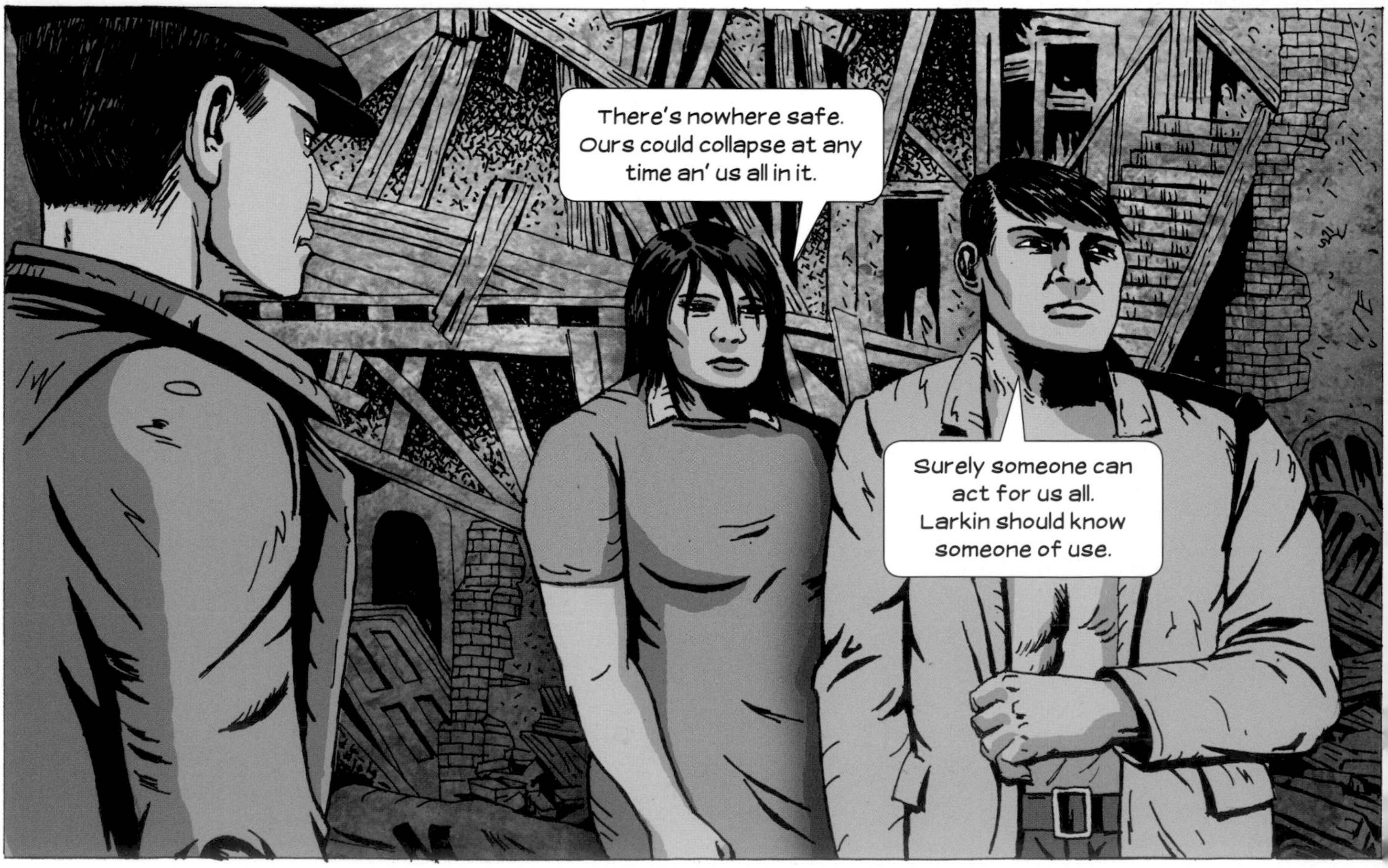
There's nowhere safe. Ours could collapse at any time an' us all in it.
Surely someone can act for us all. Larkin should know someone of use.

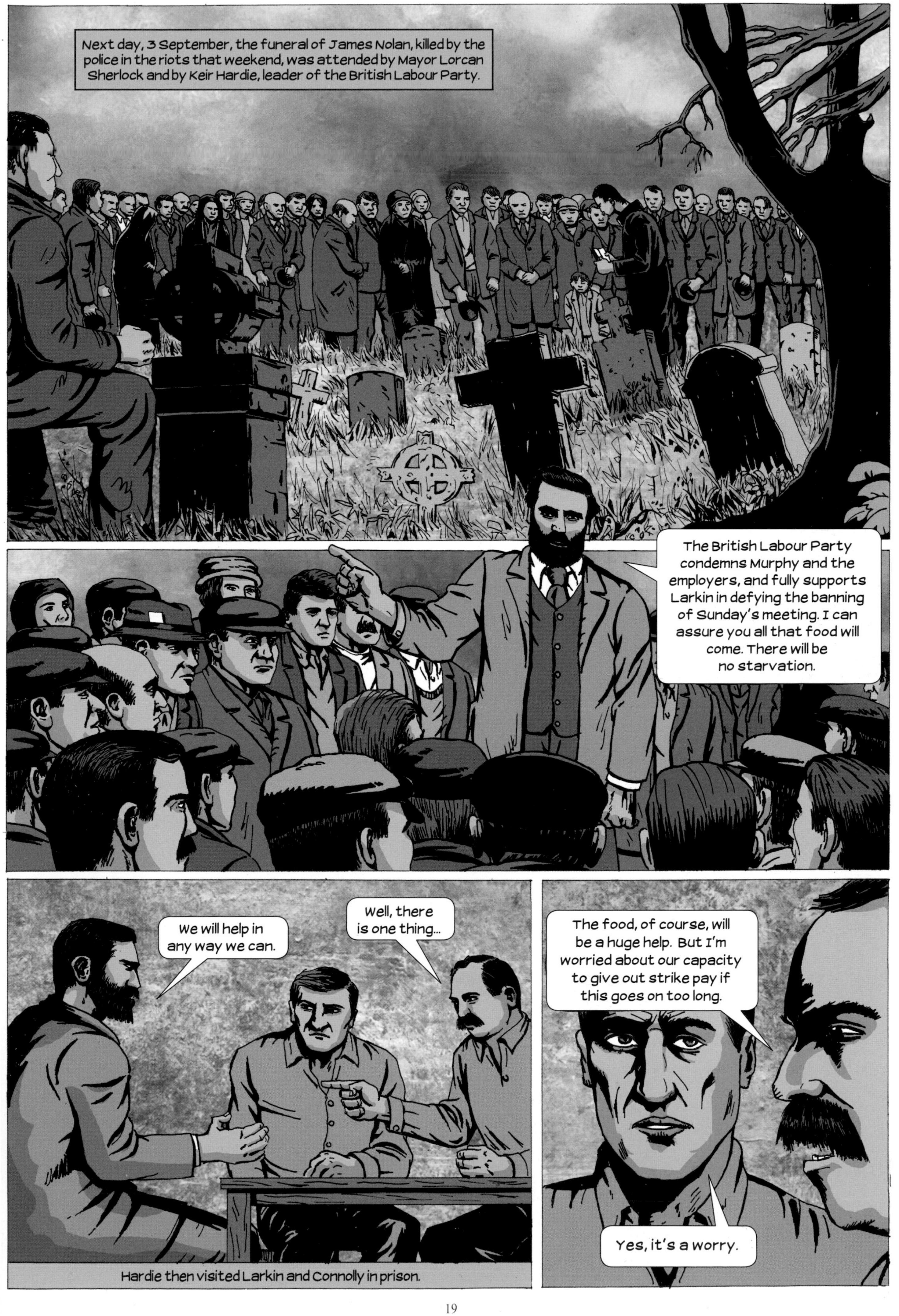

Next day, 3 September, the funeral of James Nolan, killed by the police in the riots that weekend, was attended by Mayor Lorcan Sherlock and by Keir Hardie, leader of the British Labour Party.
The British Labour Party condemns Murphy and the employers, and fully supports Larkin in defying the banning of Sunday's meeting. I can assure you all that food will come. There will be no starvation.
We will help in any way we can.
Well, there is one thing...
Hardie then visited Larkin and Connolly in prison.
The food, of course, will be a huge help. But I'm worried about our capacity to give out strike pay if this goes on too long.
Yes, it's a worry.

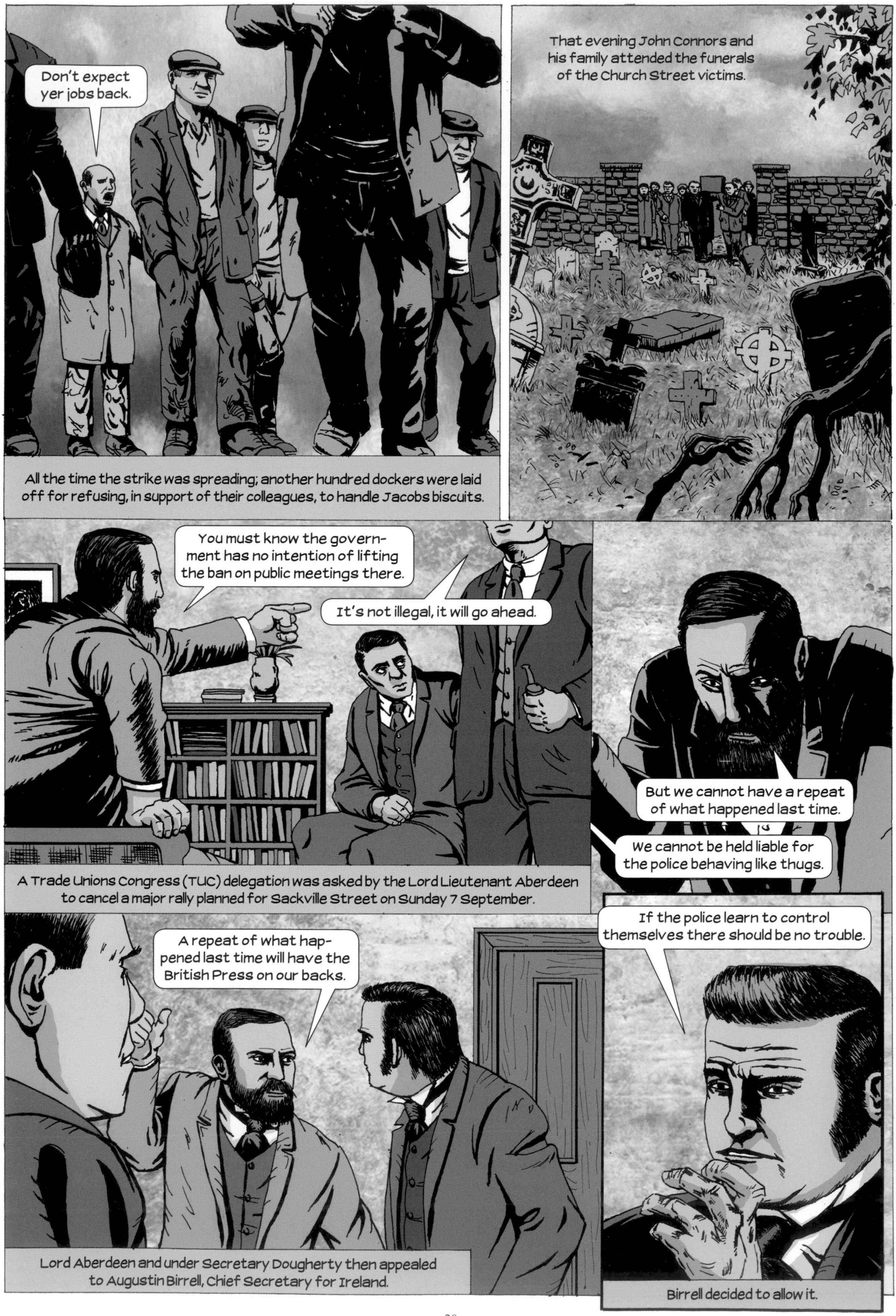
Don't expect yer jobs back.
All the time the strike was spreading; another hundred dockers were laid off for refusing, in support of their colleagues, to handle Jacobs biscuits.
That evening John Connors and his family attended the funerals of the Church Street victims.
You must know the government has no intention of lifting the ban on public meetings there.
It's not illegal, it will go ahead.
A Trade Unions Congress (TUC) delegation was asked by the Lord Lieutenant Aberdeen to cancel a major rally planned for Sackville Street on Sunday 7 September.
But we cannot have a repeat of what happened last time.
We cannot be held liable for the police behaving like thugs.
A repeat of what happened last time will have the British Press on our backs.
Lord Aberdeen and under Secretary Dougherty then appealed to Augustin Birrell, Chief Secretary for Ireland.
If the police learn to control themselves there should be no trouble.
Birrell decided to allow it.

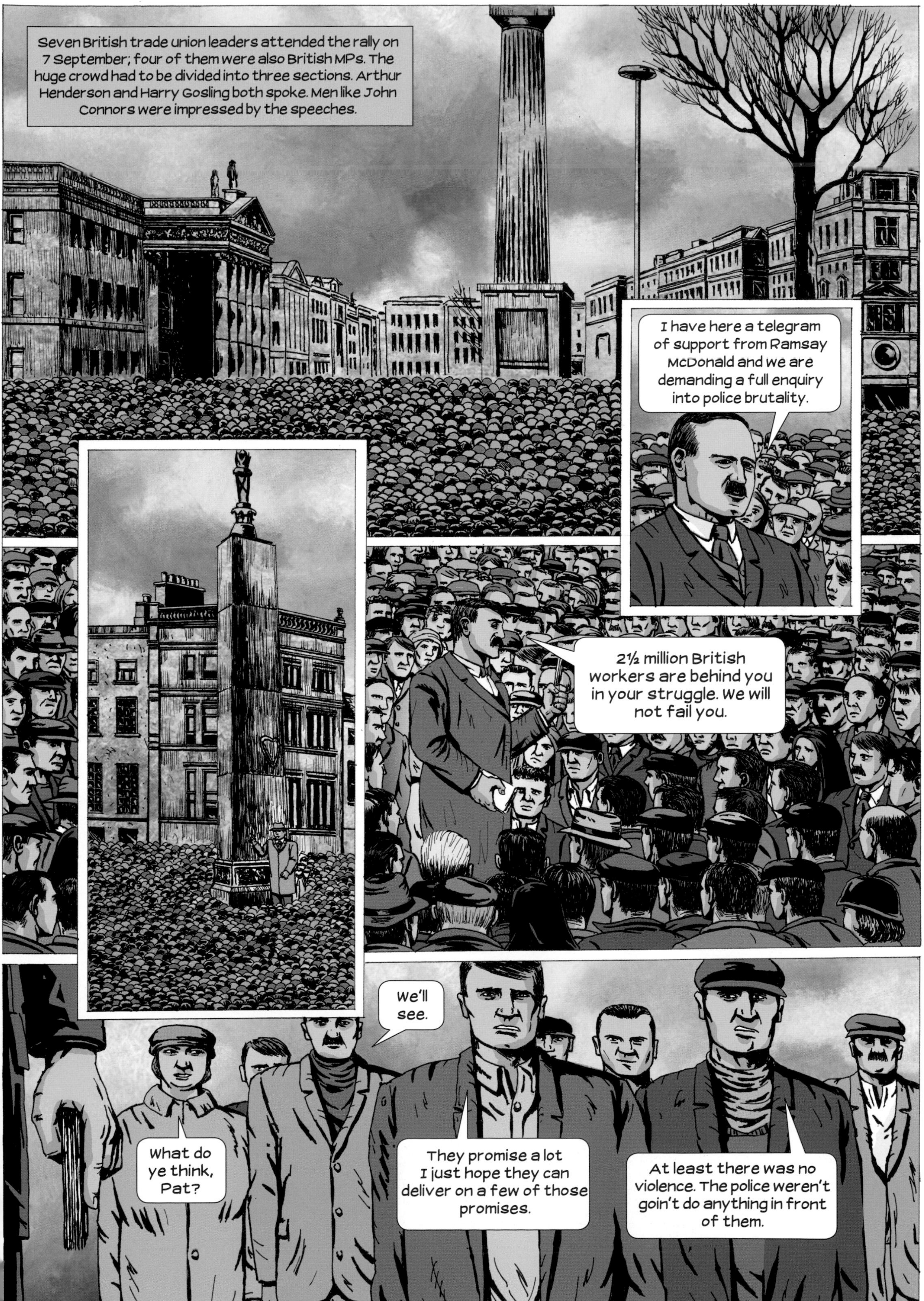
Seven British trade union leaders attended the rally on 7 September; four of them were also British MPs. The huge crowd had to be divided into three sections. Arthur Henderson and Harry Gosling both spoke. Men like John Connors were impressed by the speeches.
I have here a telegram of support from Ramsay McDonald and we are demanding a full enquiry into police brutality.
2½ million British workers are behind you in your struggle. We will not fail you.
What do ye think, Pat?
We'll see.
They promise a lot I just hope they can deliver on a few of those promises.
At least there was no violence. The police weren't goin't do anything in front of them.

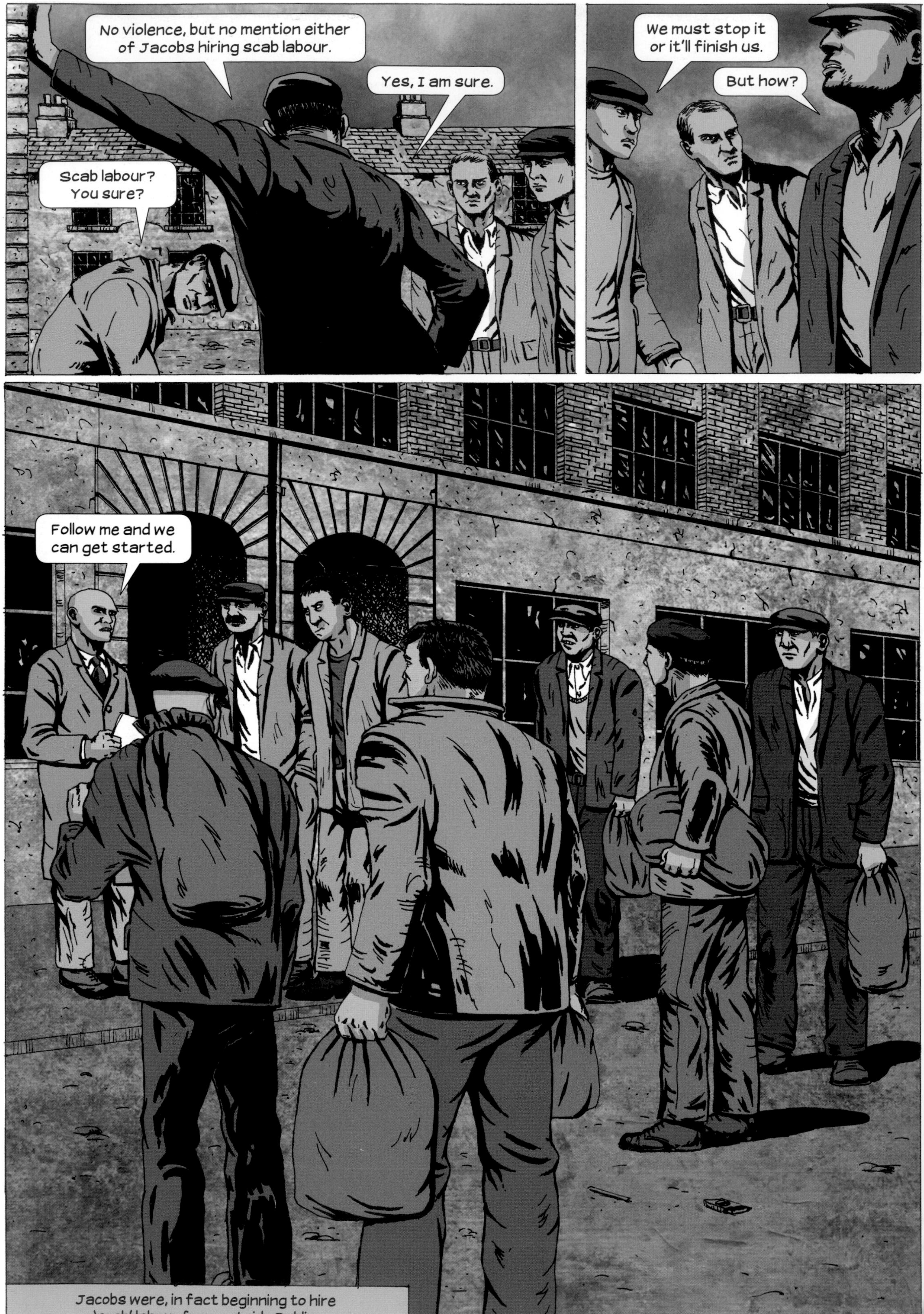

No violence, but no mention either of Jacobs hiring scab labour.
Scab labour? You sure?
Yes, I am sure.
We must stop it or it'll finish us.
But how?
Follow me and we can get started.
Jacobs were, in fact beginning to hire 'scab' labour from outside Dublin.

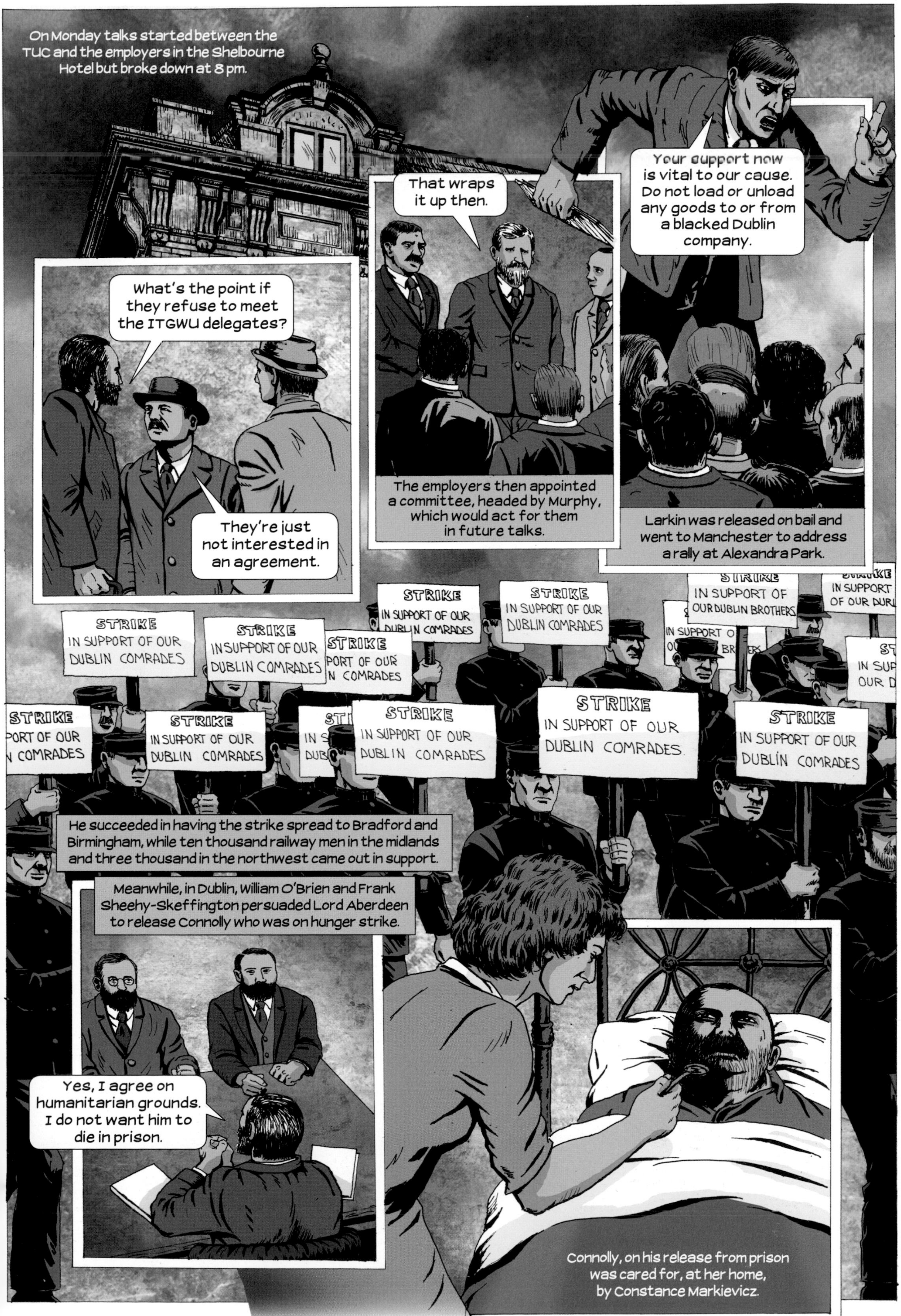
On Monday talks started between the TUC and the employers in the Shelbourne Hotel but broke down at 8 pm.
What's the point if they refuse to meet the ITGWU delegates?
They're just not interested in an agreement.
That wraps it up then.
The employers then appointed a committee, headed by Murphy, which would act for them in future talks.
Your support now is vital to our cause. Do not load or unload any goods to or from a blacked Dublin company.
Larkin was released on bail and went to Manchester to address a rally at Alexandra Park.
STRIKE IN SUPPORT OF OUR DUBLIN COMRADES
STRIKE IN SUPPORT OF OUR DUBLIN BROTHERS
He succeeded in having the strike spread to Bradford and Birmingham, while ten thousand railway men in the midlands and three thousand in the northwest came out in support.
Meanwhile, in Dublin, William O'Brien and Frank Sheehy-Skeffington persuaded Lord Aberdeen to release Connolly who was on hunger strike.
Yes, I agree on humanitarian grounds. I do not want him to die in prison.
Connolly, on his release from prison was cared for, at her home, by Constance Markievicz.

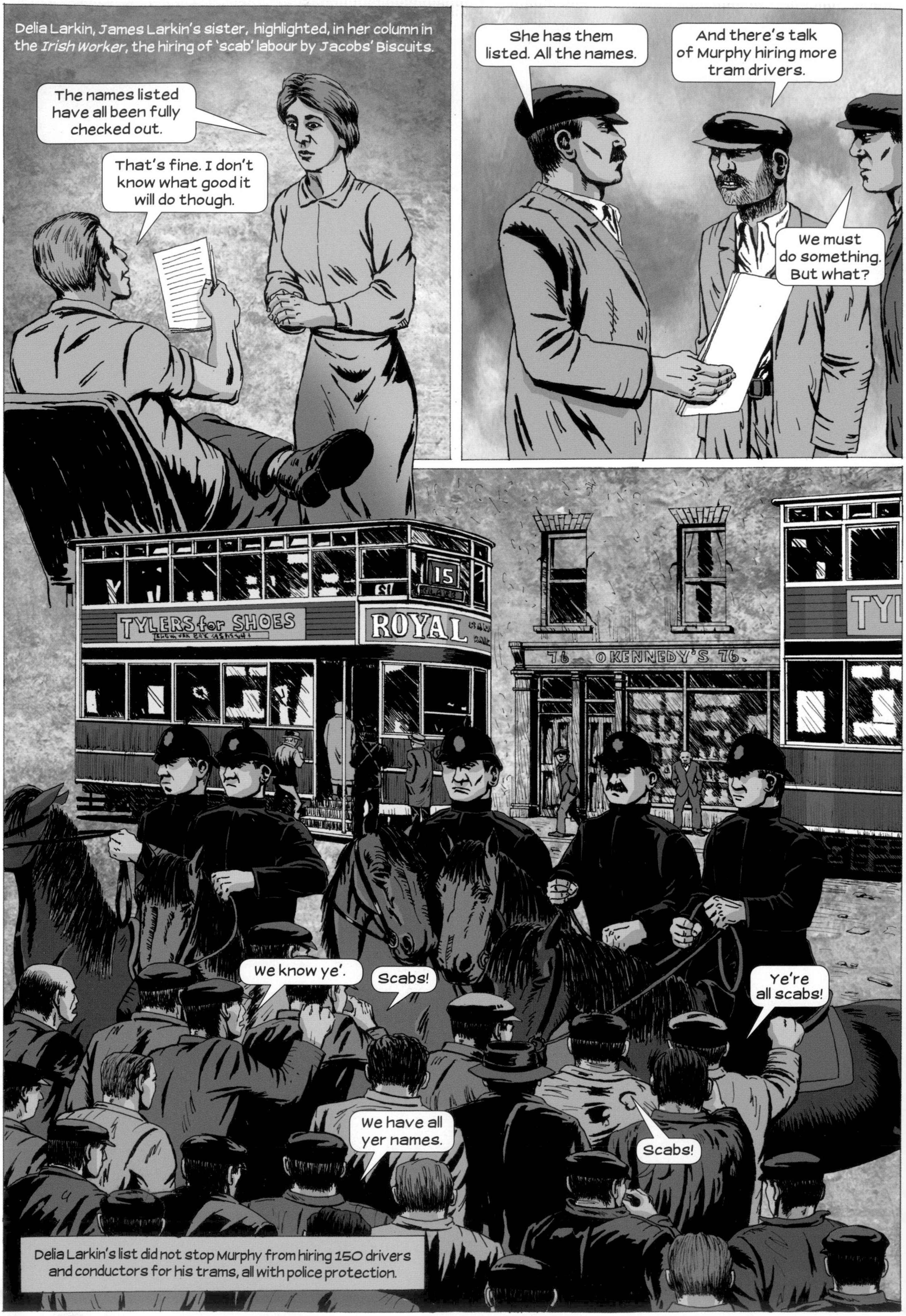
Delia Larkin, James Larkin's sister, highlighted, in her column in the *Irish Worker*, the hiring of 'scab' labour by Jacobs' Biscuits.
The names listed have all been fully checked out.
That's fine. I don't know what good it will do though.
She has them listed. All the names.
And there's talk of Murphy hiring more tram drivers.
We must do something. But what?
15
TYLERS for SHOES
ROYAL
76 OKENNEDY'S 76.
We know ye'.
Scabs!
Ye're all scabs!
We have all yer names.
Scabs!
Delia Larkin's list did not stop Murphy from hiring 150 drivers and conductors for his trams, all with police protection.

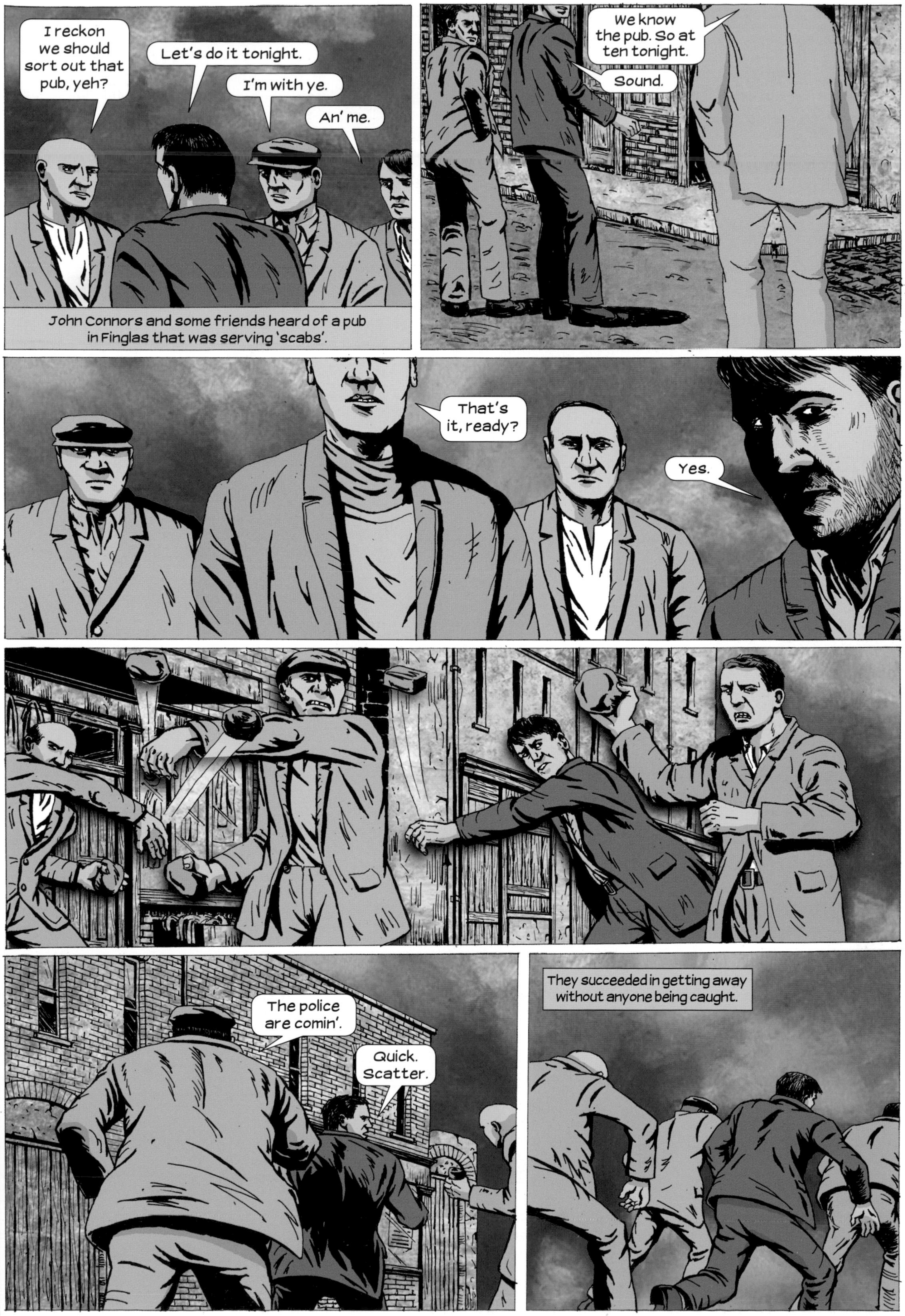
I reckon we should sort out that pub, yeh?
Let's do it tonight.
I'm with ye.
An' me.
John Connors and some friends heard of a pub in Finglas that was serving 'scabs'.
We know the pub. So at ten tonight.
Sound.
That's it, ready?
Yes.
The police are comin'.
Quick. Scatter.
They succeeded in getting away without anyone being caught.

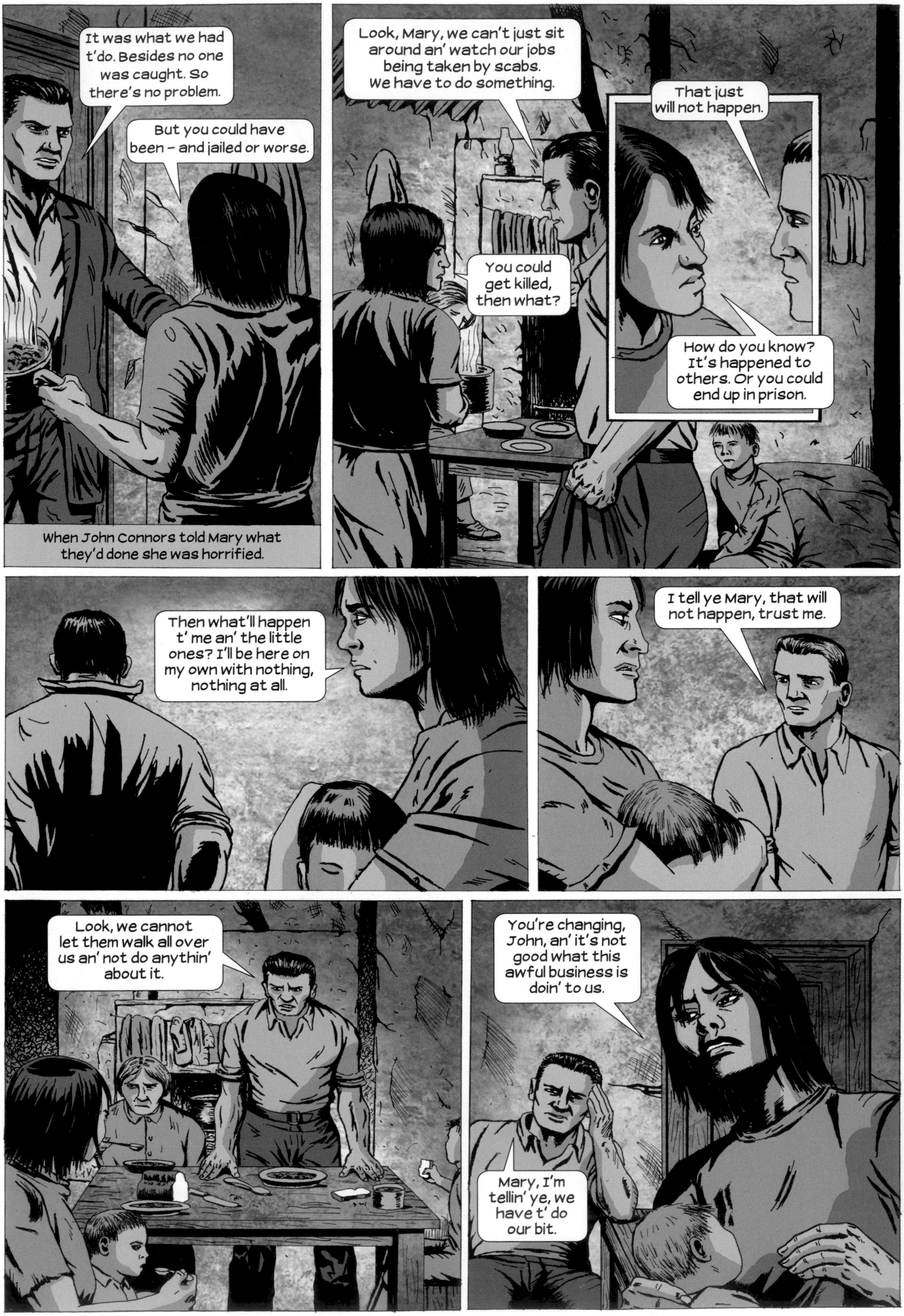
It was what we had t'do. Besides no one was caught. So there's no problem.
But you could have been – and jailed or worse.
When John Connors told Mary what they'd done she was horrified.
Look, Mary, we can't just sit around an' watch our jobs being taken by scabs. We have to do something.
You could get killed, then what?
That just will not happen.
How do you know? It's happened to others. Or you could end up in prison.
Then what'll happen t' me an' the little ones? I'll be here on my own with nothing, nothing at all.
I tell ye Mary, that will not happen, trust me.
Look, we cannot let them walk all over us an' not do anythin' about it.
You're changing, John, an' it's not good what this awful business is doin' to us.
Mary, I'm tellin' ye, we have t' do our bit.

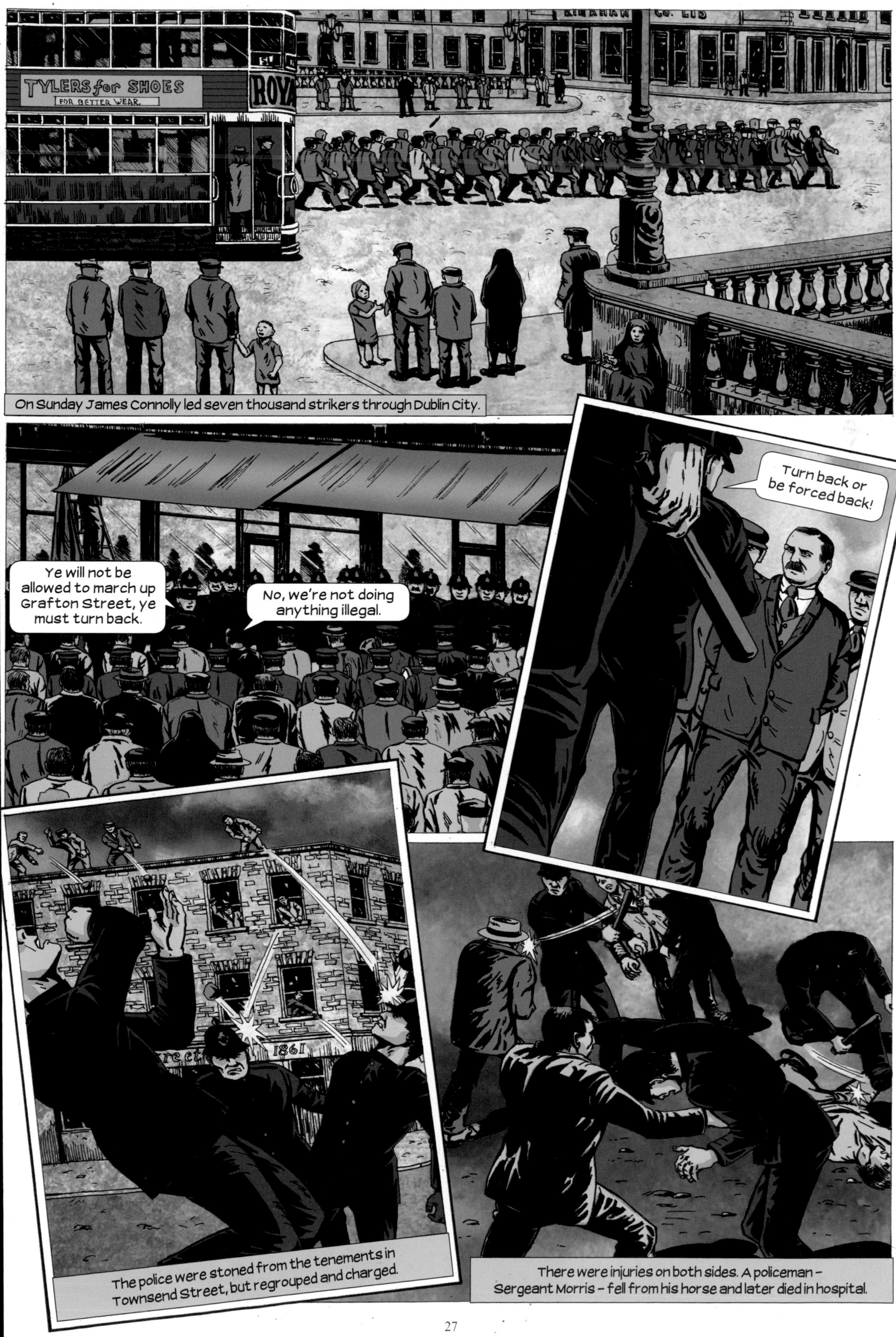
TYLERS for SHOES
FOR BETTER WEAR.
On Sunday James Connolly led seven thousand strikers through Dublin City.
Ye will not be allowed to march up Grafton Street, ye must turn back.
No, we're not doing anything illegal.
Turn back or be forced back!
The police were stoned from the tenements in Townsend Street, but regrouped and charged.
1861
There were injuries on both sides. A policeman – Sergeant Morris – fell from his horse and later died in hospital.

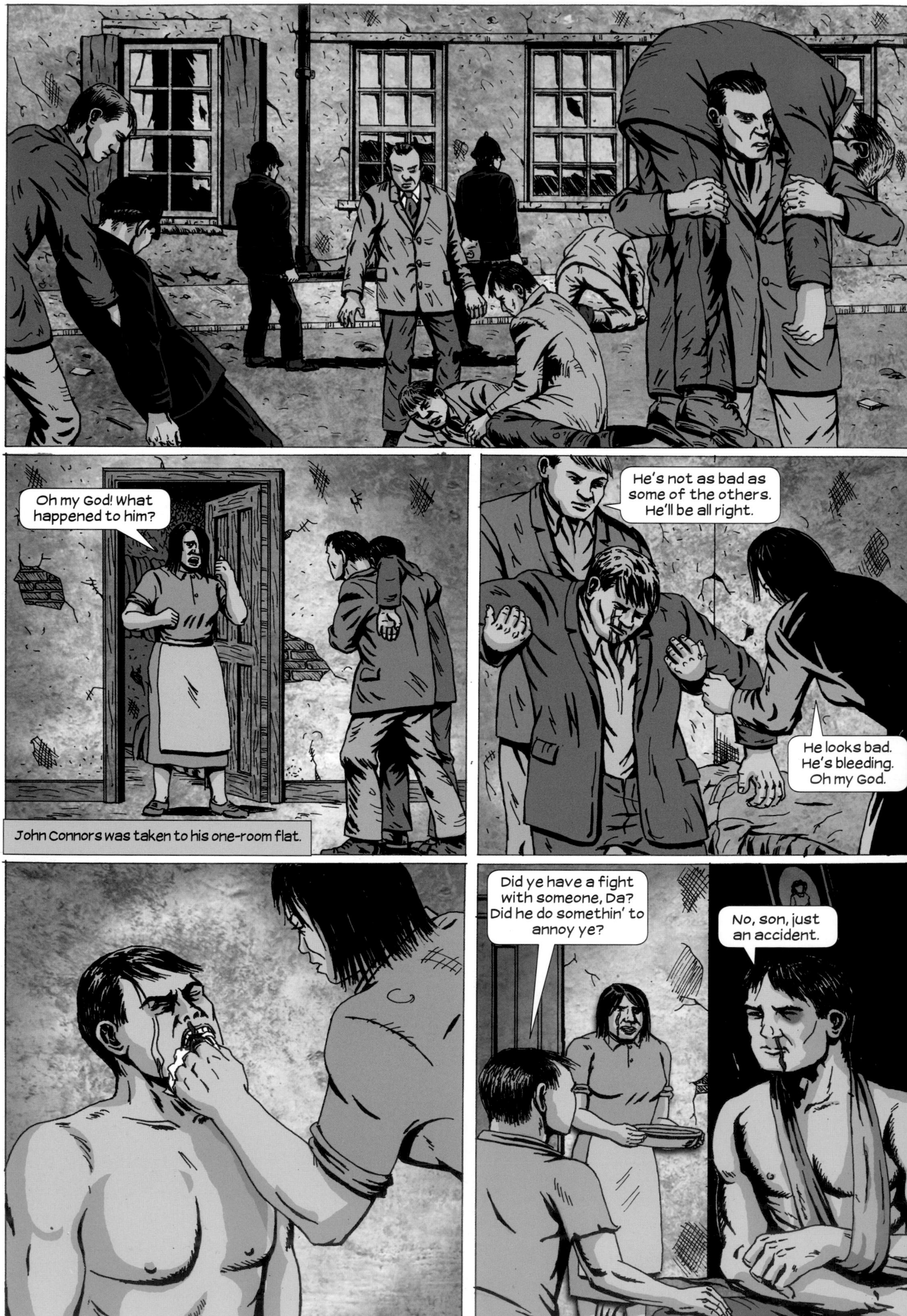
Oh my God! What happened to him?
John Connors was taken to his one-room flat.
He's not as bad as some of the others. He'll be all right.
He looks bad. He's bleeding. Oh my God.
Did ye have a fight with someone, Da? Did he do somethin' to annoy ye?
No, son, just an accident.

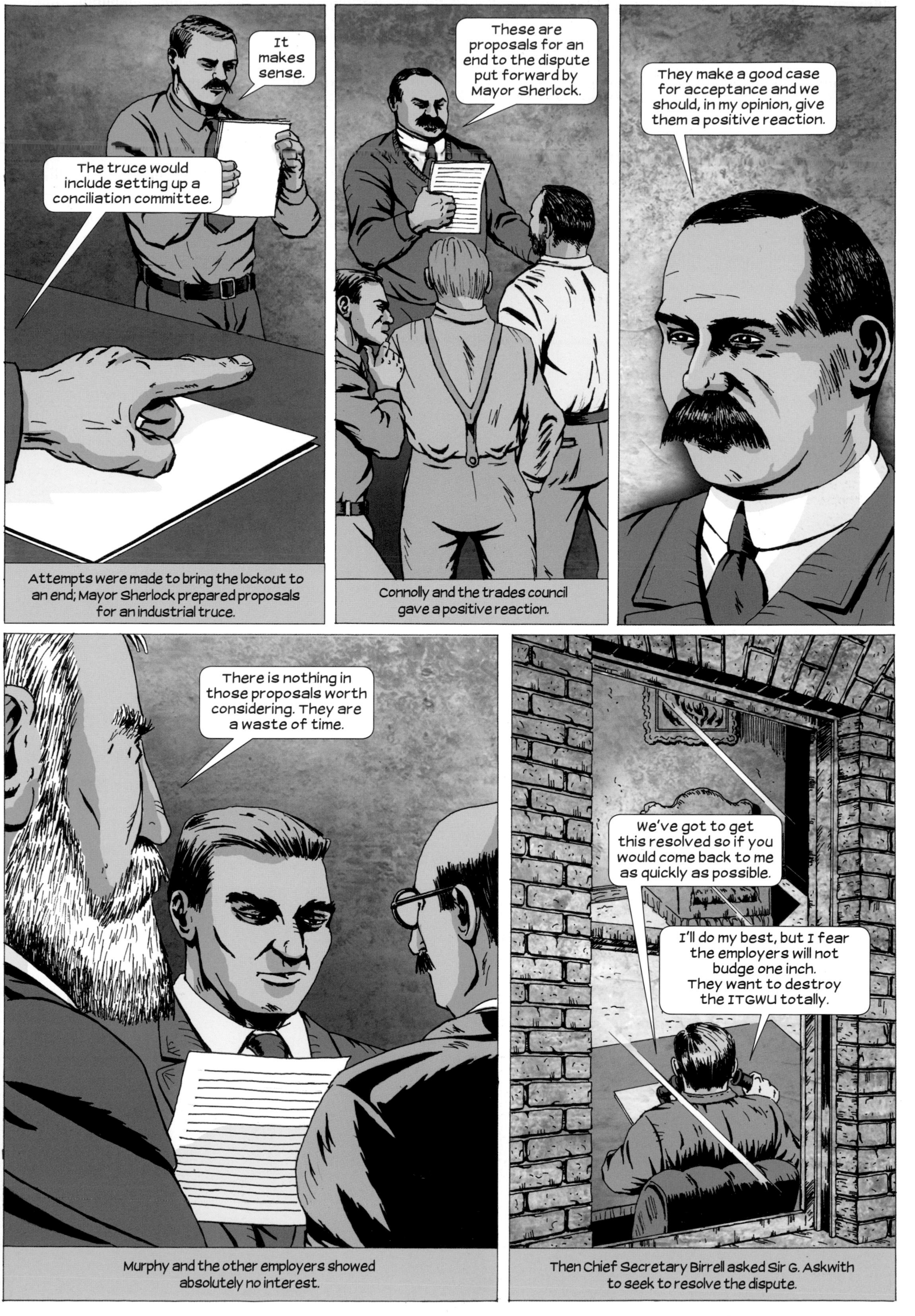
It makes sense.
The truce would include setting up a conciliation committee.
Attempts were made to bring the lockout to an end; Mayor Sherlock prepared proposals for an industrial truce.
These are proposals for an end to the dispute put forward by Mayor Sherlock.
Connolly and the trades council gave a positive reaction.
They make a good case for acceptance and we should, in my opinion, give them a positive reaction.
There is nothing in those proposals worth considering. They are a waste of time.
Murphy and the other employers showed absolutely no interest.
We've got to get this resolved so if you would come back to me as quickly as possible.
I'll do my best, but I fear the employers will not budge one inch. They want to destroy the ITGWU totally.
Then Chief Secretary Birrell asked Sir G. Askwith to seek to resolve the dispute.

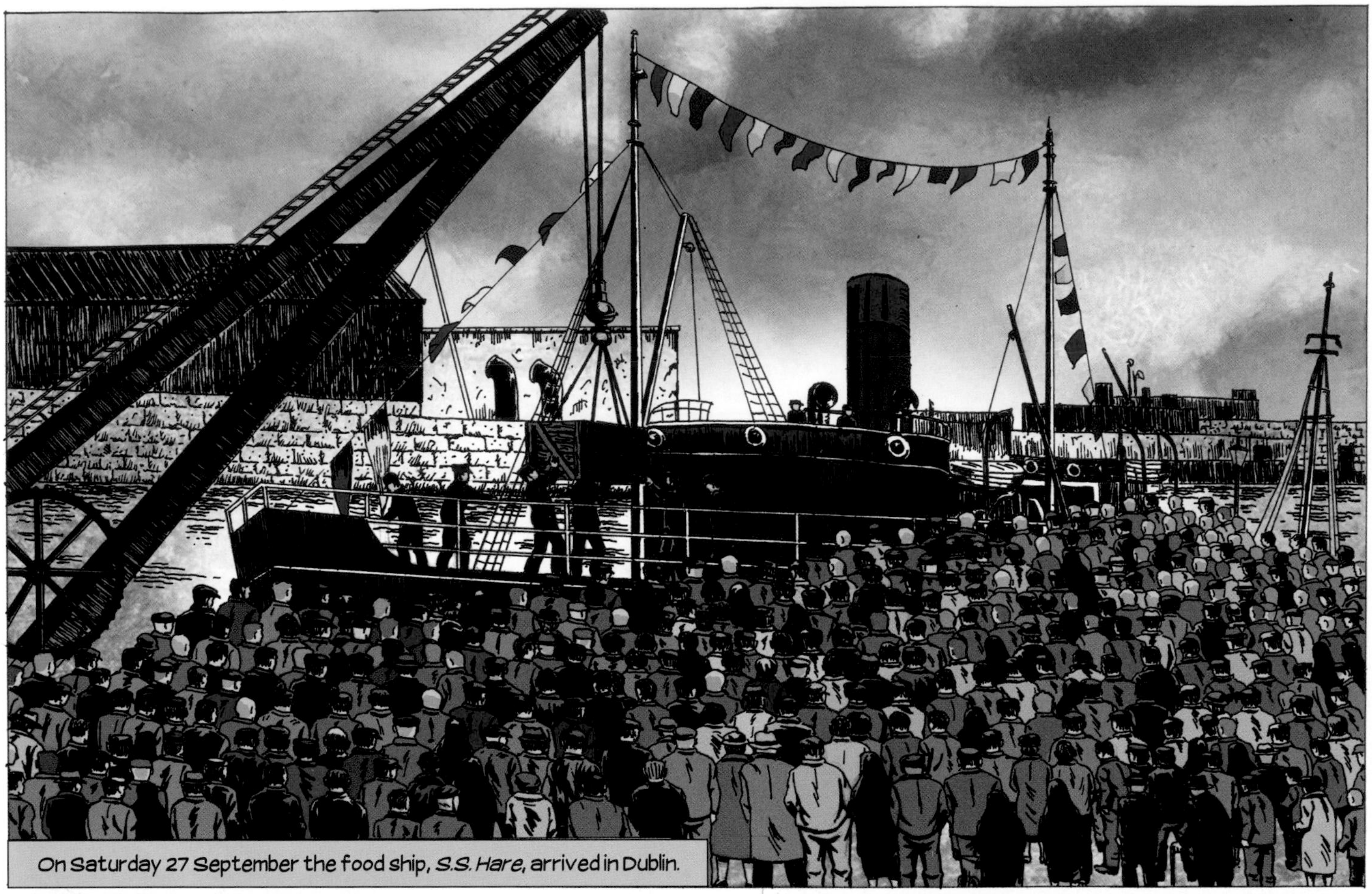
On Saturday 27 September the food ship, *S.S. Hare*, arrived in Dublin.

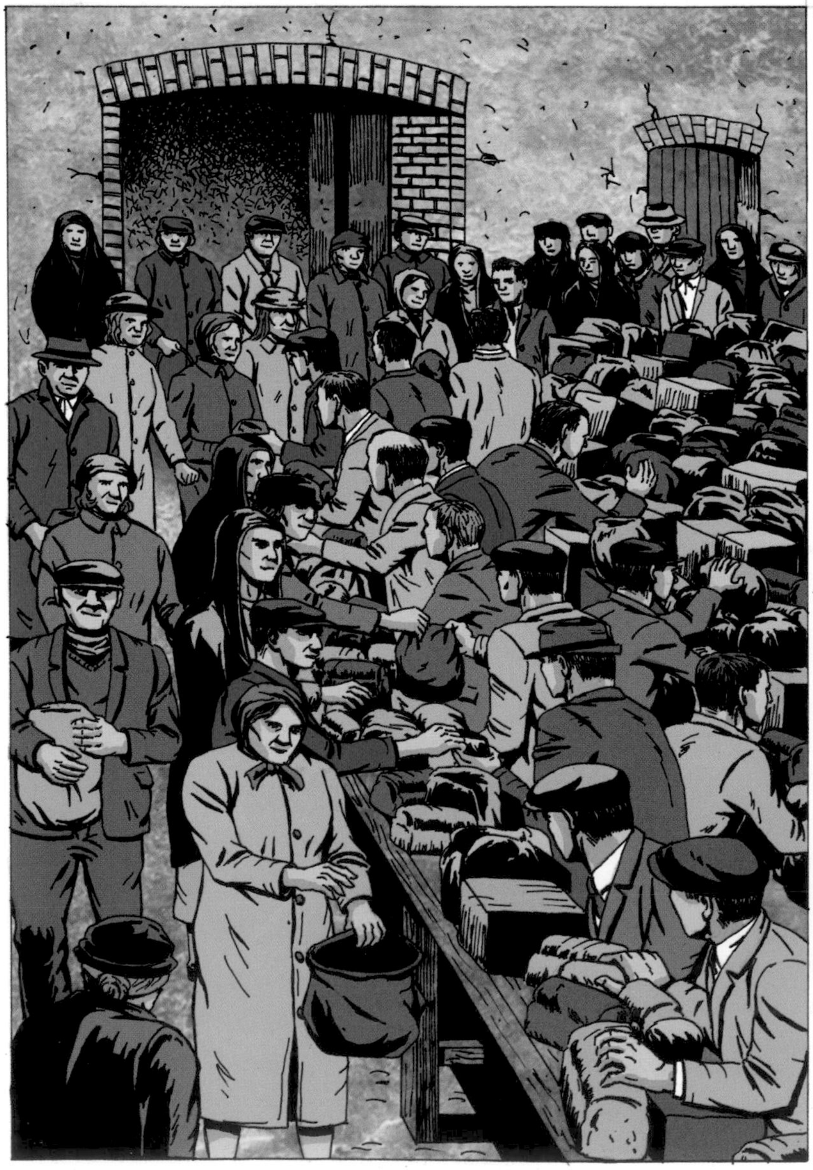

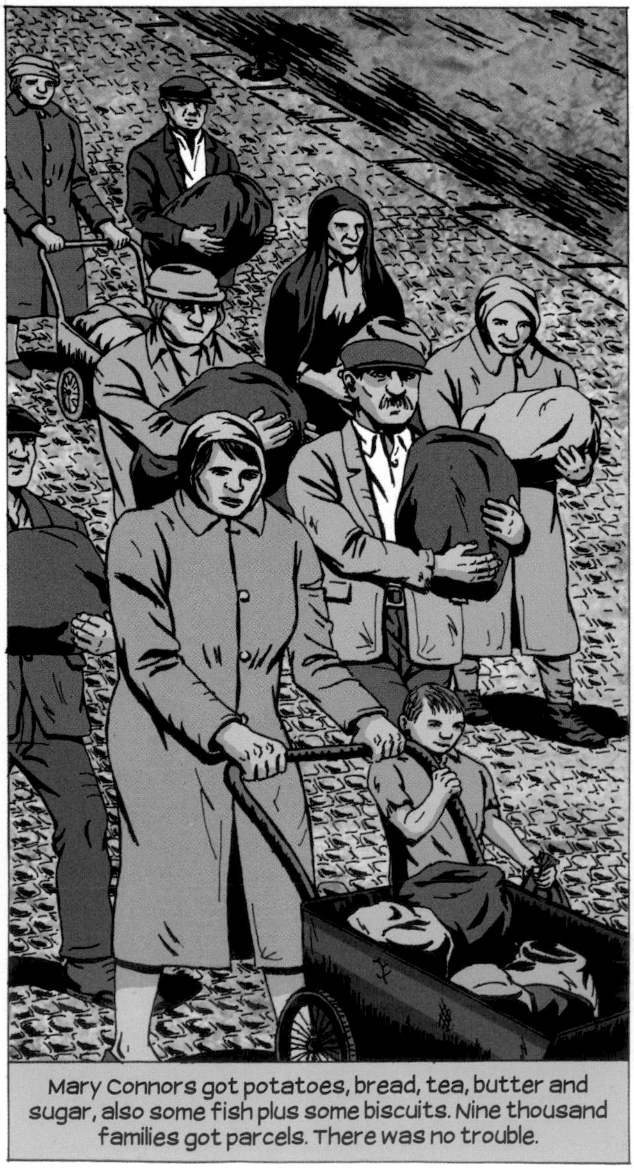
Mary Connors got potatoes, bread, tea, butter and sugar, also some fish plus some biscuits. Nine thousand families got parcels. There was no trouble.

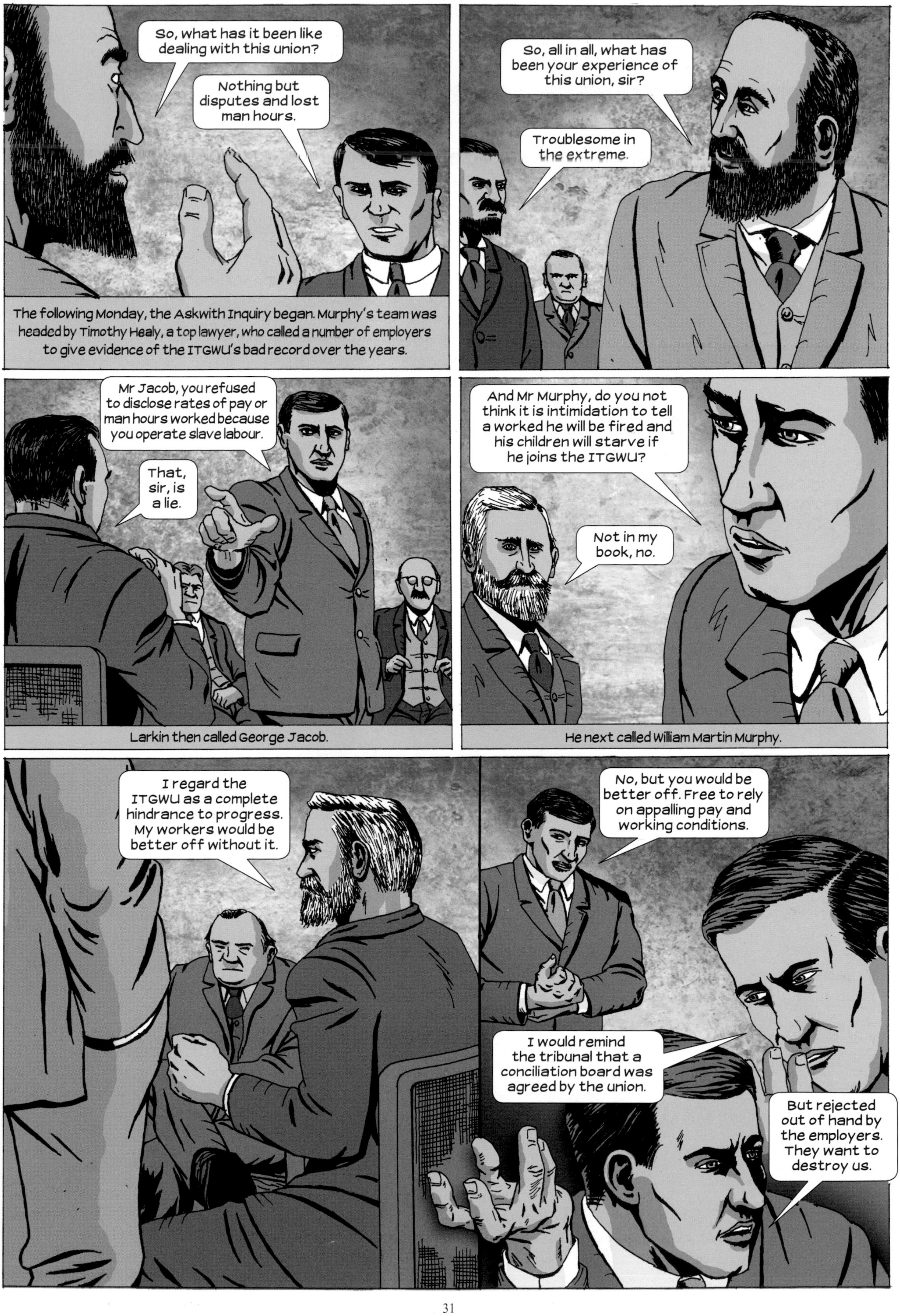
So, what has it been like dealing with this union?
Nothing but disputes and lost man hours.
The following Monday, the Askwith Inquiry began. Murphy's team was headed by Timothy Healy, a top lawyer, who called a number of employers to give evidence of the ITGWU's bad record over the years.
So, all in all, what has been your experience of this union, sir?
Troublesome in the extreme.
Mr Jacob, you refused to disclose rates of pay or man hours worked because you operate slave labour.
That, sir, is a lie.
Larkin then called George Jacob.
And Mr Murphy, do you not think it is intimidation to tell a worked he will be fired and his children will starve if he joins the ITGWU?
Not in my book, no.
He next called William Martin Murphy.
I regard the ITGWU as a complete hindrance to progress. My workers would be better off without it.
No, but you would be better off. Free to rely on appalling pay and working conditions.
I would remind the tribunal that a conciliation board was agreed by the union.
But rejected out of hand by the employers. They want to destroy us.

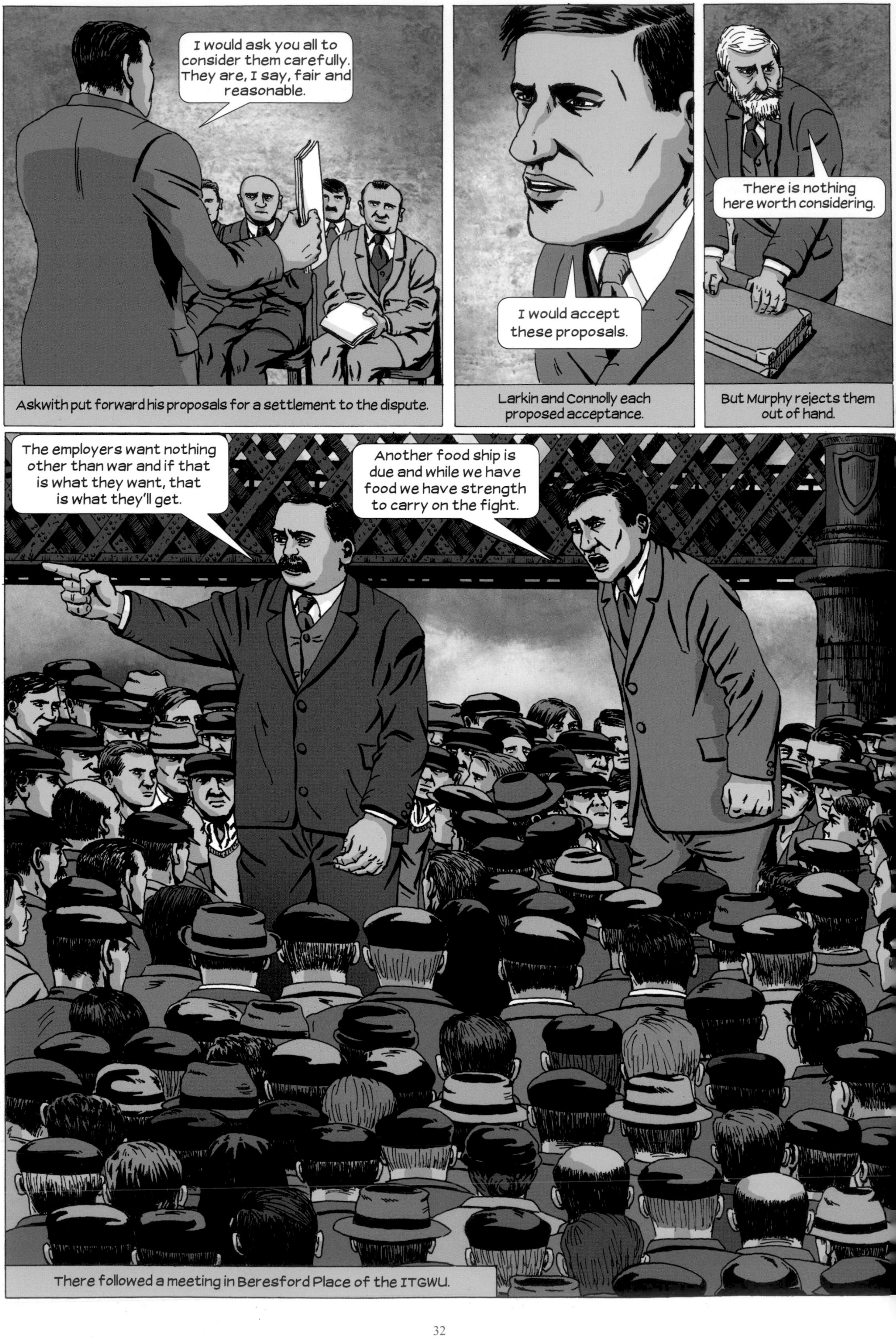
I would ask you all to consider them carefully. They are, I say, fair and reasonable.
Askwith put forward his proposals for a settlement to the dispute.
I would accept these proposals.
Larkin and Connolly each proposed acceptance.
There is nothing here worth considering.
But Murphy rejects them out of hand.
The employers want nothing other than war and if that is what they want, that is what they'll get.
Another food ship is due and while we have food we have strength to carry on the fight.
There followed a meeting in Beresford Place of the ITGWU.

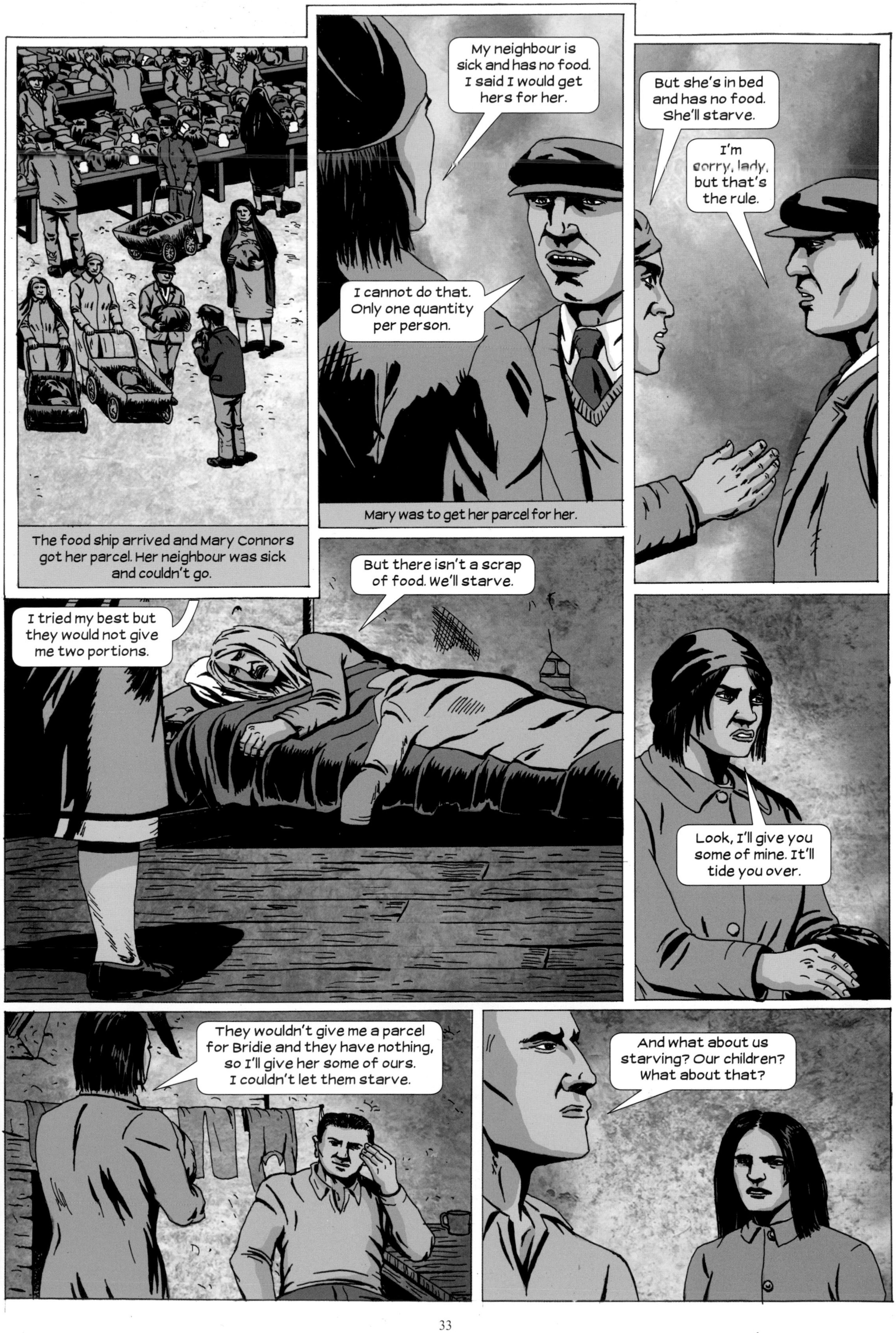

The food ship arrived and Mary Connors got her parcel. Her neighbour was sick and couldn't go.
My neighbour is sick and has no food. I said I would get hers for her.
I cannot do that. Only one quantity per person.
Mary was to get her parcel for her.
But she's in bed and has no food. She'll starve.
I'm sorry, lady, but that's the rule.
I tried my best but they would not give me two portions.
But there isn't a scrap of food. We'll starve.
Look, I'll give you some of mine. It'll tide you over.
They wouldn't give me a parcel for Bridie and they have nothing, so I'll give her some of ours. I couldn't let them starve.
And what about us starving? Our children? What about that?

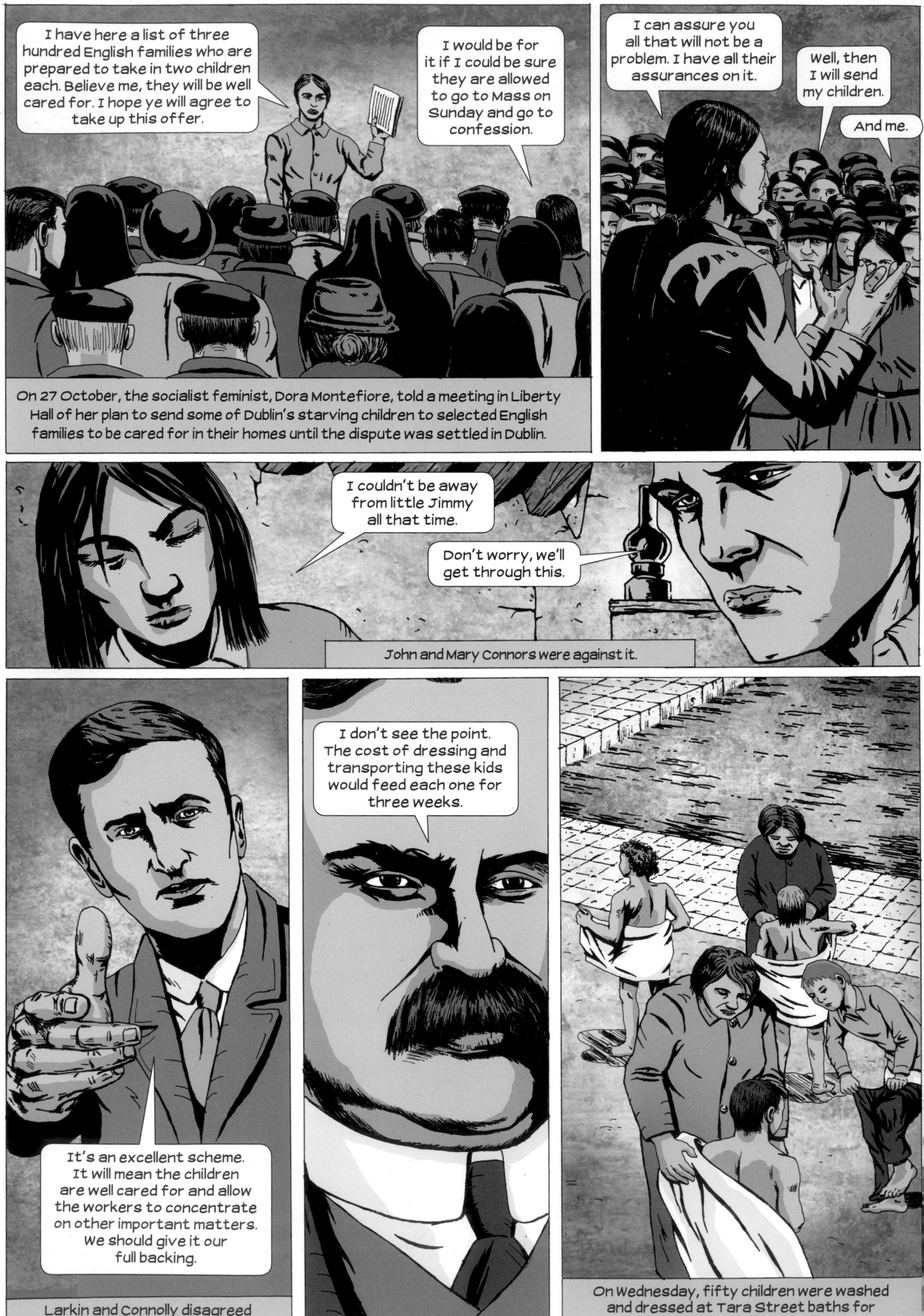
I have here a list of three hundred English families who are prepared to take in two children each. Believe me, they will be well cared for. I hope ye will agree to take up this offer.
I would be for it if I could be sure they are allowed to go to Mass on Sunday and go to confession.
On 27 October, the socialist feminist, Dora Montefiore, told a meeting in Liberty Hall of her plan to send some of Dublin's starving children to selected English families to be cared for in their homes until the dispute was settled in Dublin.
I can assure you all that will not be a problem. I have all their assurances on it.
Well, then I will send my children.
And me.
I couldn't be away from little Jimmy all that time.
Don't worry, we'll get through this.
John and Mary Connors were against it.
It's an excellent scheme. It will mean the children are well cared for and allow the workers to concentrate on other important matters. We should give it our full backing.
Larkin and Connolly disagreed on the whole plan.
I don't see the point. The cost of dressing and transporting these kids would feed each one for three weeks.
On Wednesday, fifty children were washed and dressed at Tara Street baths for the journey to England.

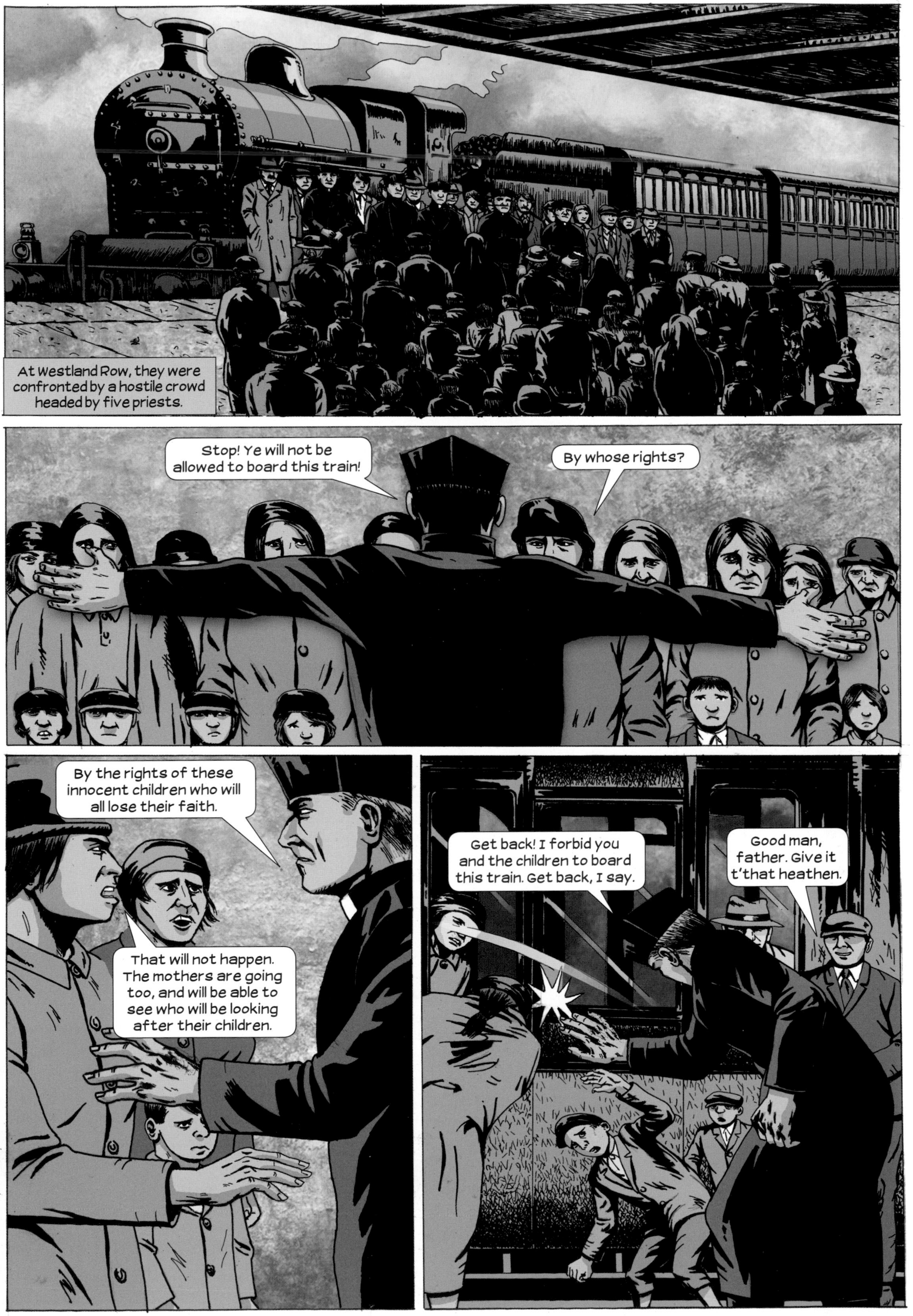

At Westland Row, they were confronted by a hostile crowd headed by five priests.
Stop! Ye will not be allowed to board this train!
By whose rights?
By the rights of these innocent children who will all lose their faith.
That will not happen. The mothers are going too, and will be able to see who will be looking after their children.
Get back! I forbid you and the children to board this train. Get back, I say.
Good man, father. Give it t'that heathen.

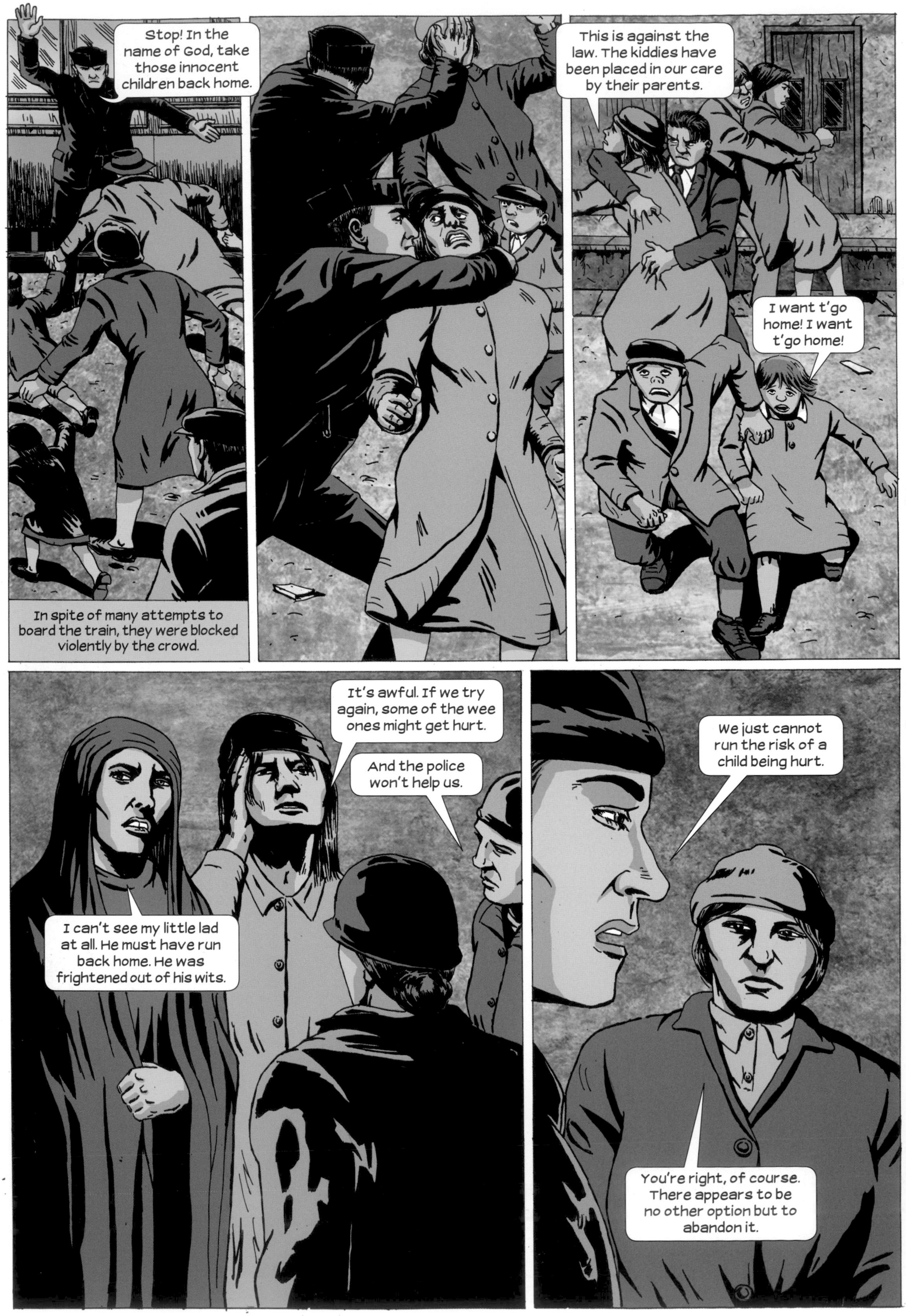
Stop! In the name of God, take those innocent children back home.
In spite of many attempts to board the train, they were blocked violently by the crowd.
This is against the law. The kiddies have been placed in our care by their parents.
I want t'go home! I want t'go home!
It's awful. If we try again, some of the wee ones might get hurt.
And the police won't help us.
I can't see my little lad at all. He must have run back home. He was frightened out of his wits.
We just cannot run the risk of a child being hurt.
You're right, of course. There appears to be no other option but to abandon it.

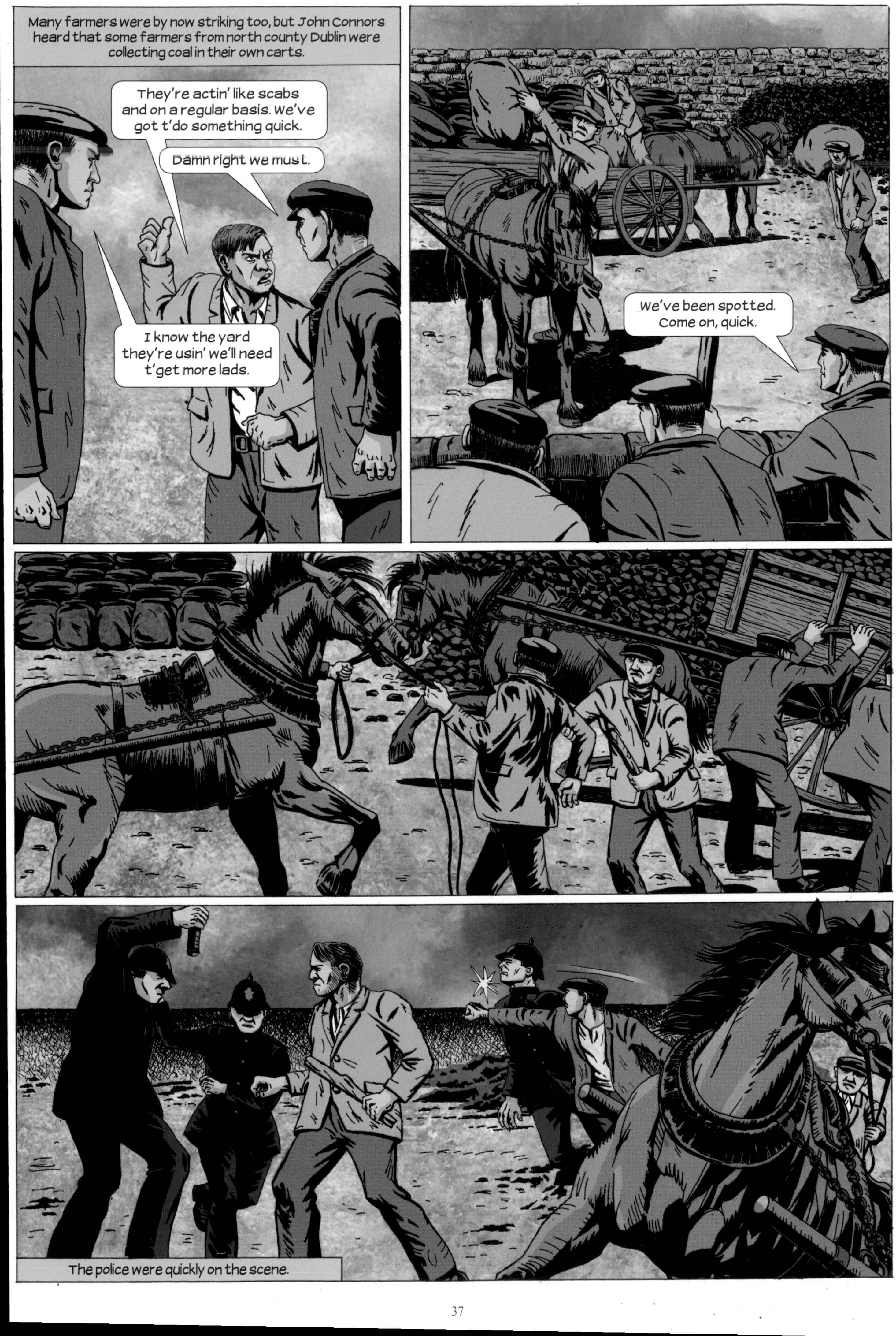

Many farmers were by now striking too, but John Connors heard that some farmers from north county Dublin were collecting coal in their own carts.
They're actin' like scabs and on a regular basis. We've got t'do something quick.
Damn right we must.
I know the yard they're usin' we'll need t'get more lads.
We've been spotted. Come on, quick.
The police were quickly on the scene.

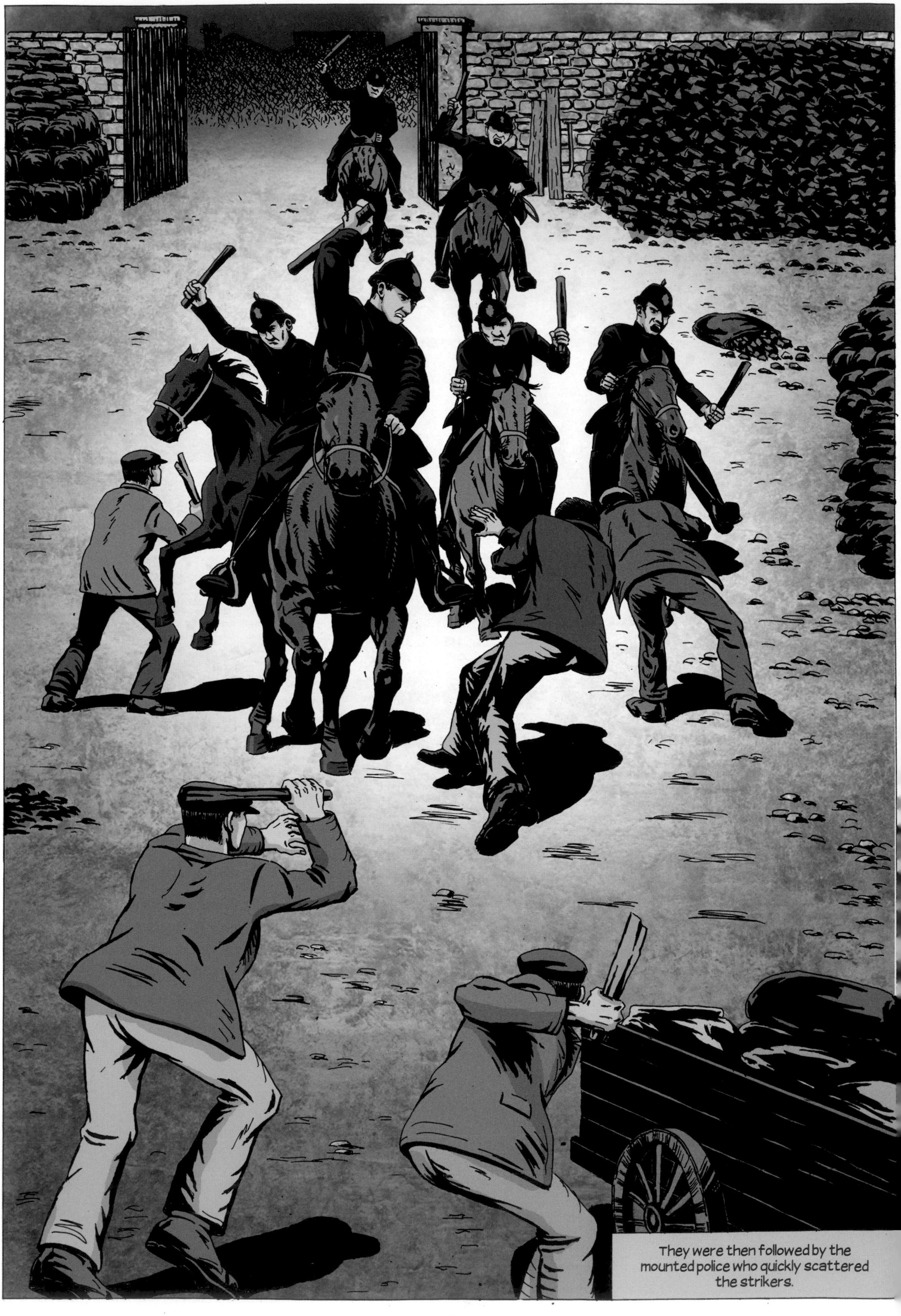
They were then followed by the mounted police who quickly scattered the strikers.

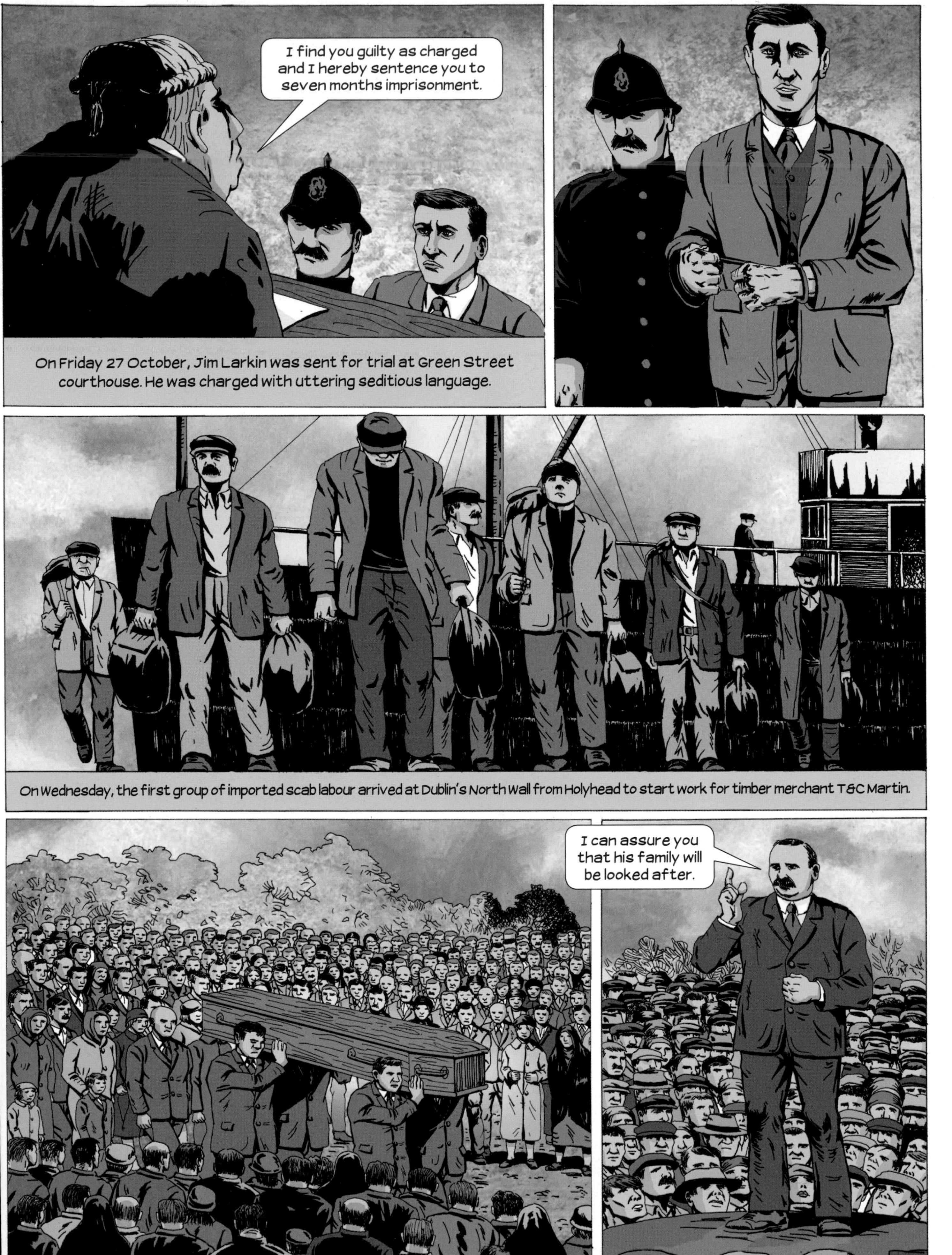
I find you guilty as charged and I hereby sentence you to seven months imprisonment.
On Friday 27 October, Jim Larkin was sent for trial at Green Street courthouse. He was charged with uttering seditious language.
On Wednesday, the first group of imported scab labour arrived at Dublin's North Wall from Holyhead to start work for timber merchant T&C Martin.
James Byrne, Branch Secretary of Kingstown ITGWU who had been on hunger strike, died of pneumonia in Mountjoy on 1 November, leaving a wife and six children. Three thousand people marched in his funeral.
I can assure you that his family will be looked after.
Connolly, standing on top of a car, told the crowd he had been murdered by being thrown into a cold, damp cell in his weak condition. He assured them that the fight would go on.

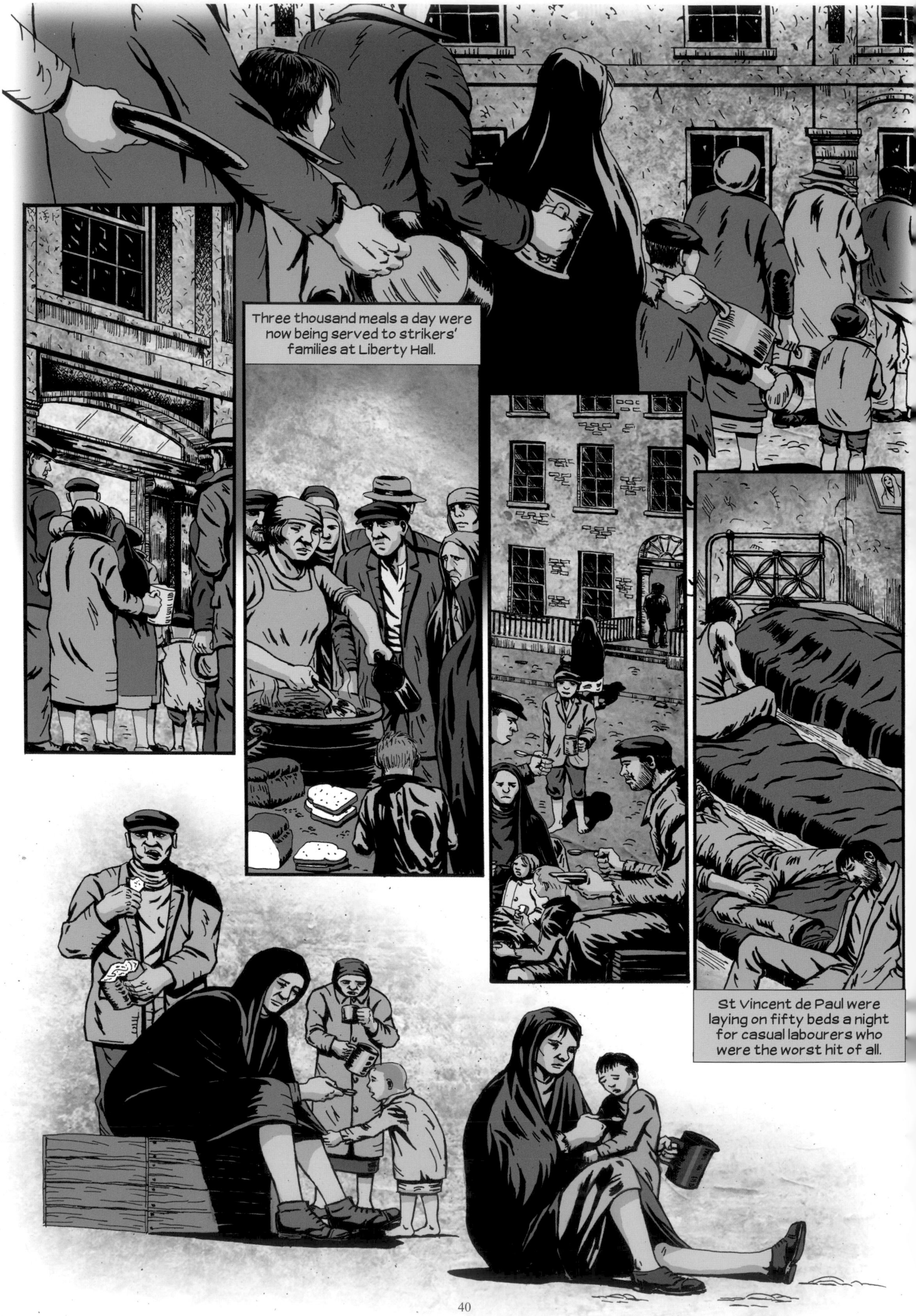
Three thousand meals a day were now being served to strikers' families at Liberty Hall.
St Vincent de Paul were laying on fifty beds a night for casual labourers who were the worst hit of all.

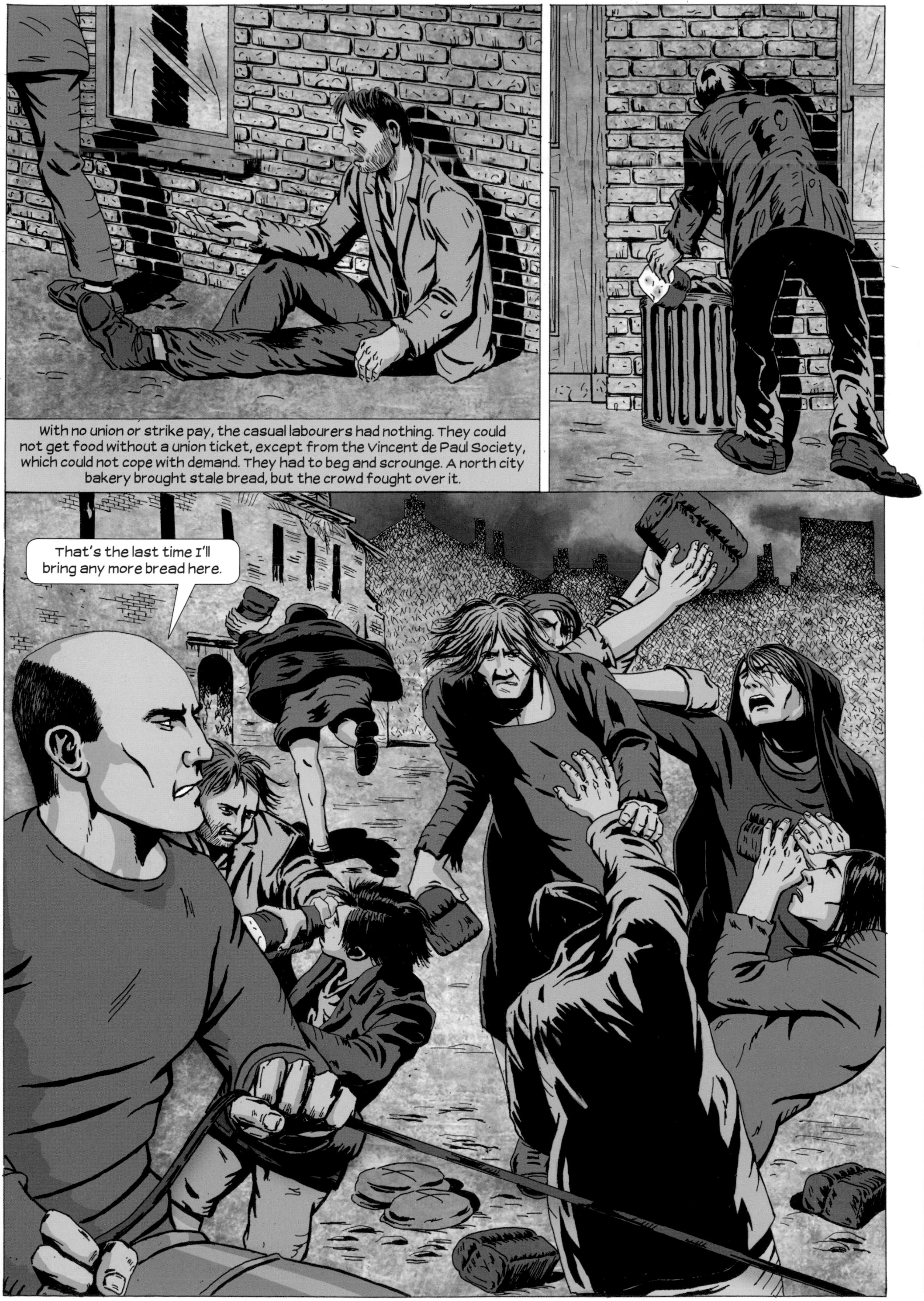
With no union or strike pay, the casual labourers had nothing. They could not get food without a union ticket, except from the Vincent de Paul Society, which could not cope with demand. They had to beg and scrounge. A north city bakery brought stale bread, but the crowd fought over it.
That's the last time I'll bring any more bread here.

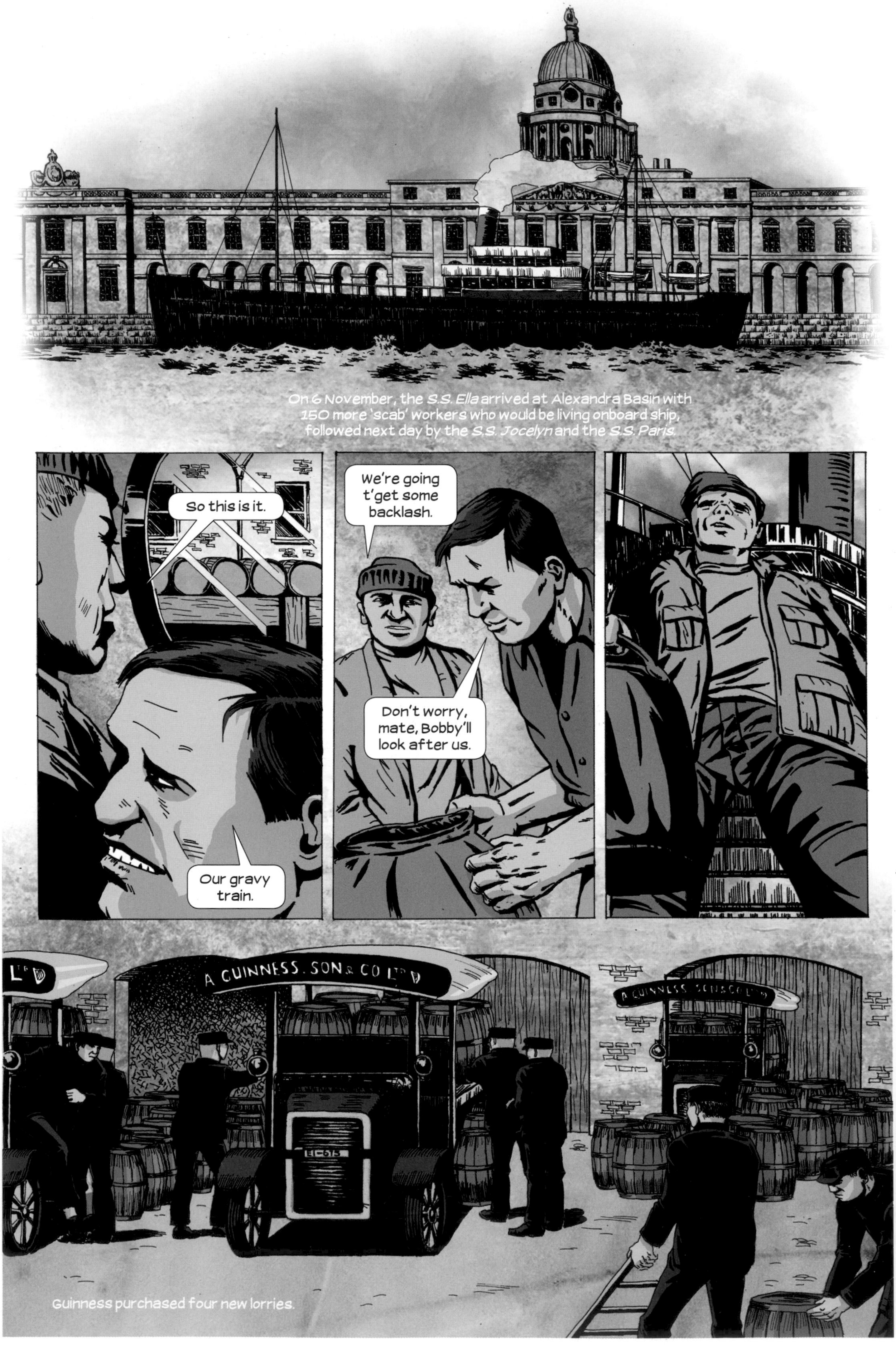

On 6 November, the S.S. Ella arrived at Alexandra Basin with 150 more 'scab' workers who would be living onboard ship, followed next day by the S.S. Jocelyn and the S.S. Paris.
So this is it.
Our gravy train.
We're going t'get some backlash.
Don't worry, mate, Bobby'll look after us.
A GUINNESS. SON & CO Ltd
Guinness purchased four new lorries.

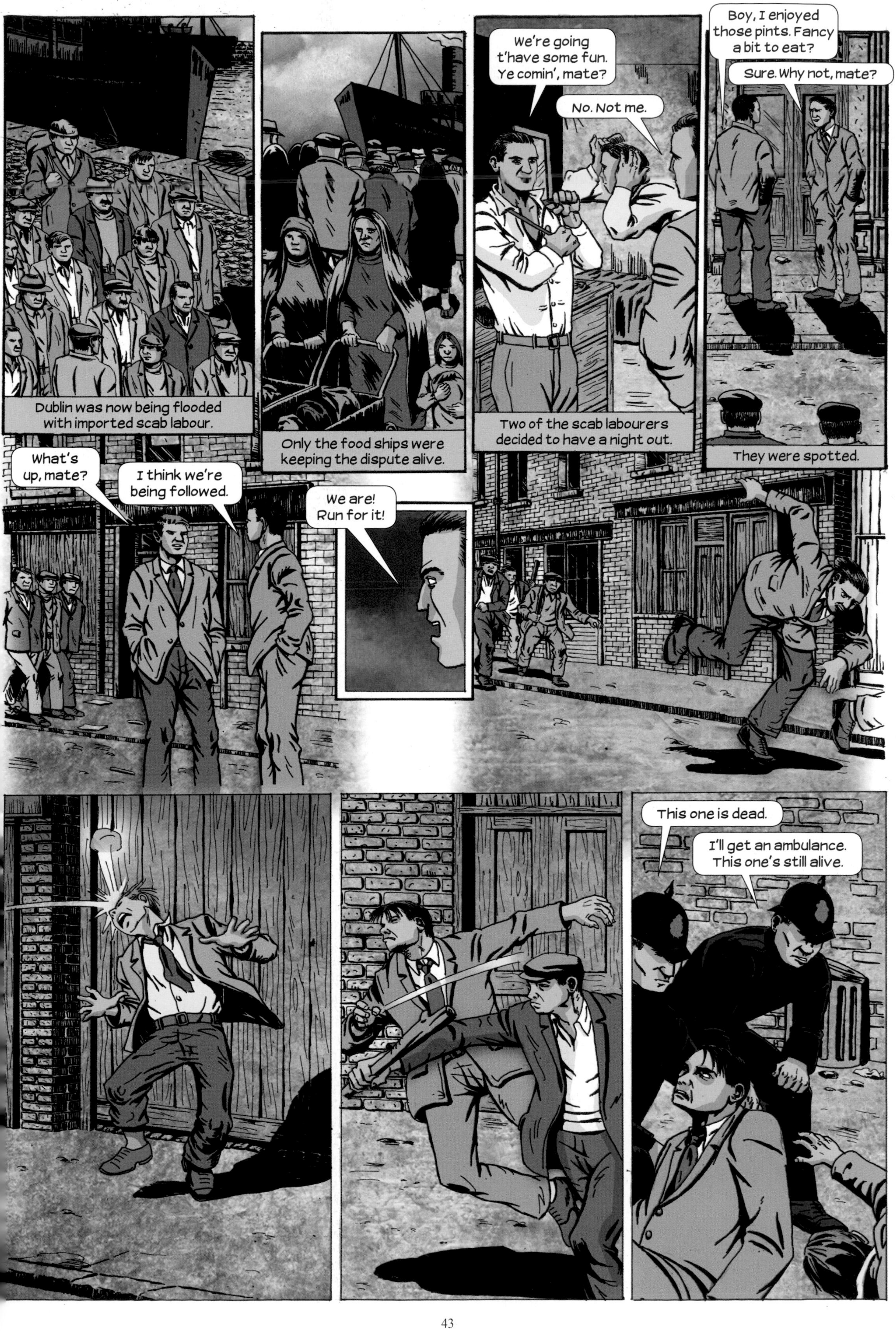
Dublin was now being flooded with imported scab labour.
Only the food ships were keeping the dispute alive.
We're going t'have some fun. Ye comin', mate?
No. Not me.
Two of the scab labourers decided to have a night out.
Boy, I enjoyed those pints. Fancy a bit to eat?
Sure. Why not, mate?
They were spotted.
What's up, mate?
I think we're being followed.
We are! Run for it!
This one is dead.
I'll get an ambulance. This one's still alive.

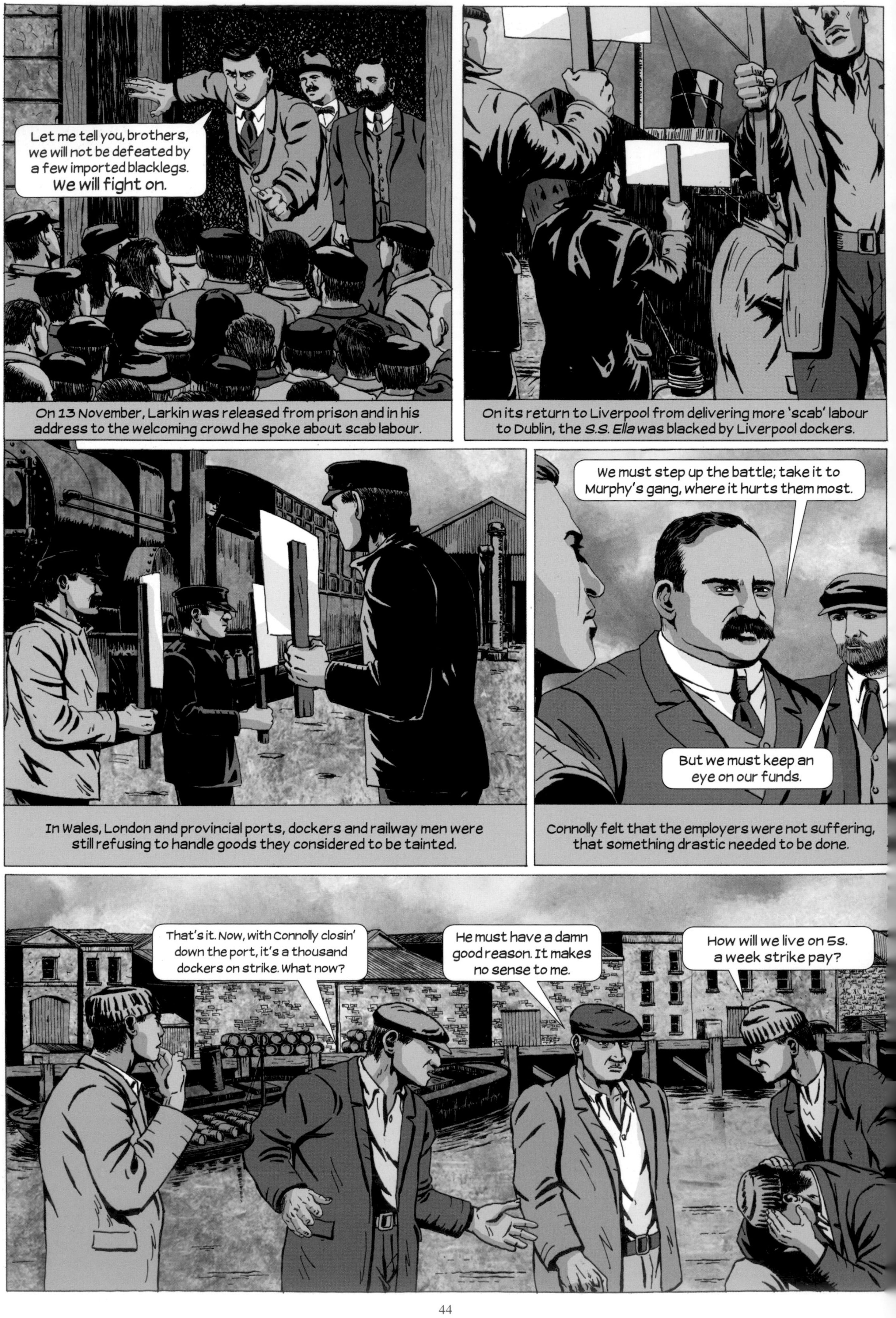
Let me tell you, brothers, we will not be defeated by a few imported blacklegs. We will fight on.
On 13 November, Larkin was released from prison and in his address to the welcoming crowd he spoke about scab labour.
On its return to Liverpool from delivering more 'scab' labour to Dublin, the *S.S. Ella* was blacked by Liverpool dockers.
In Wales, London and provincial ports, dockers and railway men were still refusing to handle goods they considered to be tainted.
We must step up the battle; take it to Murphy's gang, where it hurts them most.
But we must keep an eye on our funds.
Connolly felt that the employers were not suffering, that something drastic needed to be done.
That's it. Now, with Connolly closin' down the port, it's a thousand dockers on strike. What now?
He must have a damn good reason. It makes no sense to me.
How will we live on 5s. a week strike pay?

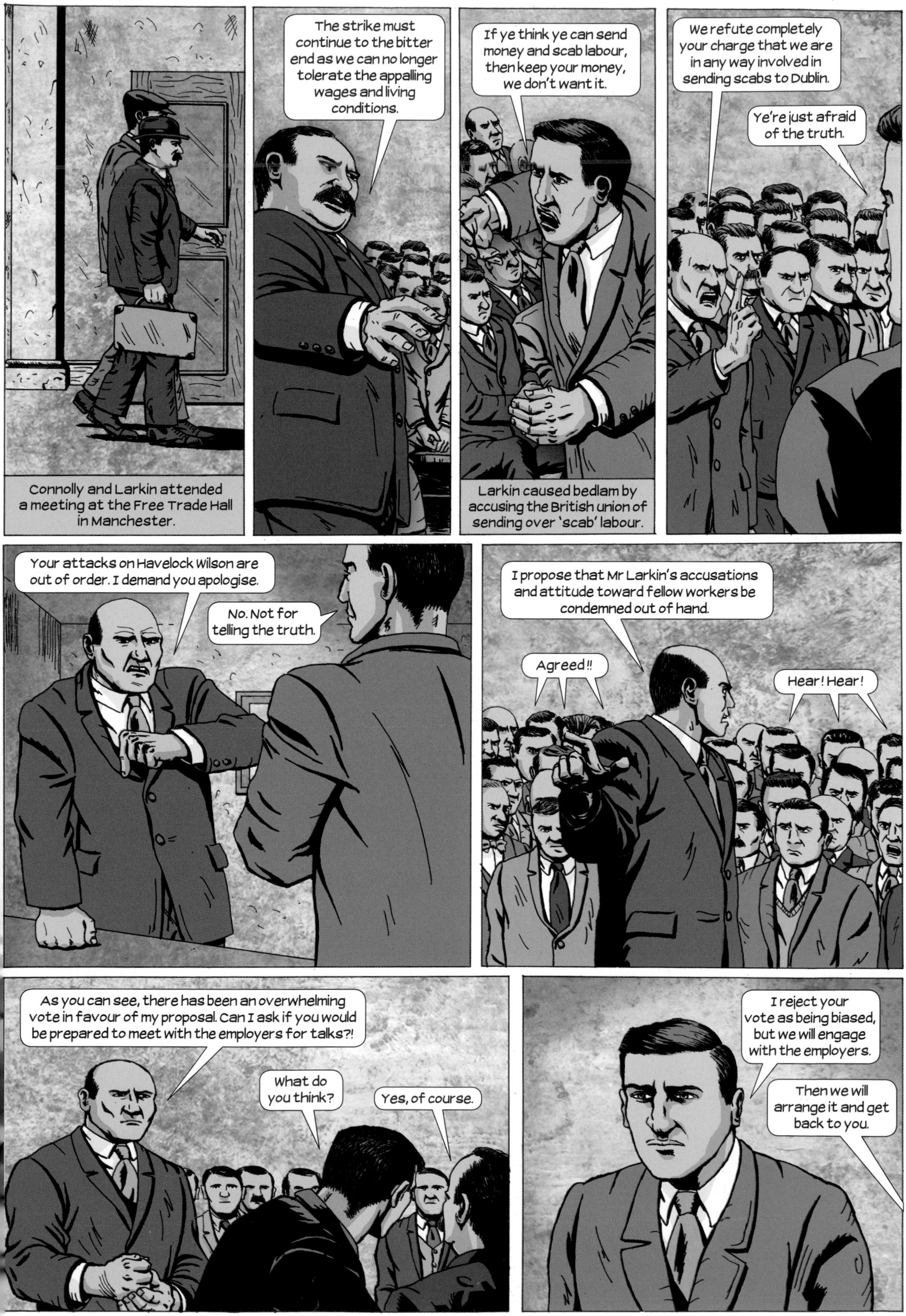

Connolly and Larkin attended a meeting at the Free Trade Hall in Manchester.
The strike must continue to the bitter end as we can no longer tolerate the appalling wages and living conditions.
If ye think ye can send money and scab labour, then keep your money, we don't want it.
Larkin caused bedlam by accusing the British union of sending over 'scab' labour.
We refute completely your charge that we are in any way involved in sending scabs to Dublin.
Ye're just afraid of the truth.
Your attacks on Havelock Wilson are out of order. I demand you apologise.
No. Not for telling the truth.
I propose that Mr Larkin's accusations and attitude toward fellow workers be condemned out of hand.
Agreed!!
Hear! Hear!
As you can see, there has been an overwhelming vote in favour of my proposal. Can I ask if you would be prepared to meet with the employers for talks?!
What do you think?
Yes, of course.
I reject your vote as being biased, but we will engage with the employers.
Then we will arrange it and get back to you.

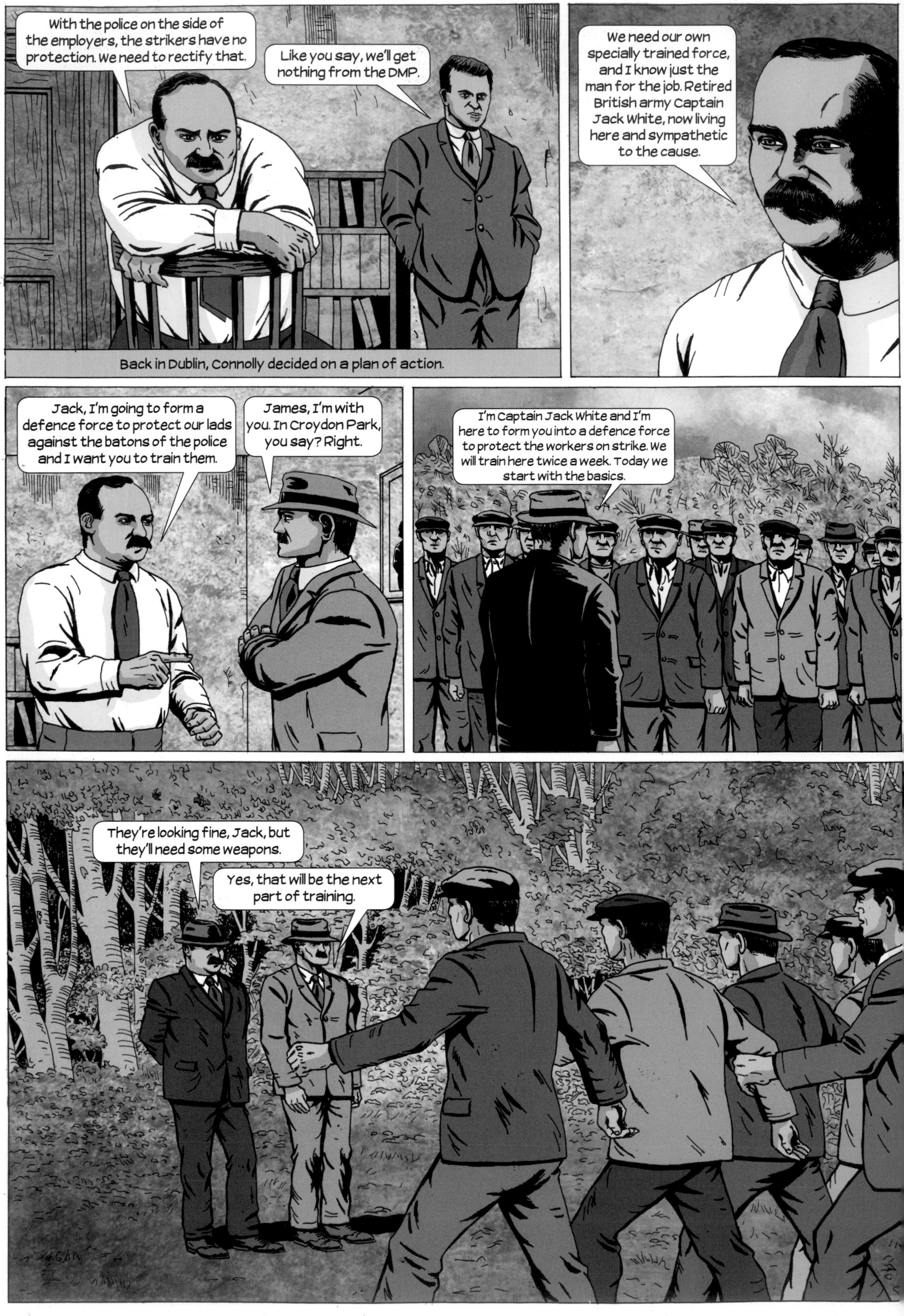
With the police on the side of the employers, the strikers have no protection. We need to rectify that.
Like you say, we'll get nothing from the DMP.
Back in Dublin, Connolly decided on a plan of action.
We need our own specially trained force, and I know just the man for the job. Retired British army Captain Jack White, now living here and sympathetic to the cause.
Jack, I'm going to form a defence force to protect our lads against the batons of the police and I want you to train them.
James, I'm with you. In Croydon Park, you say? Right.
I'm Captain Jack White and I'm here to form you into a defence force to protect the workers on strike. We will train here twice a week. Today we start with the basics.
They're looking fine, Jack, but they'll need some weapons.
Yes, that will be the next part of training.

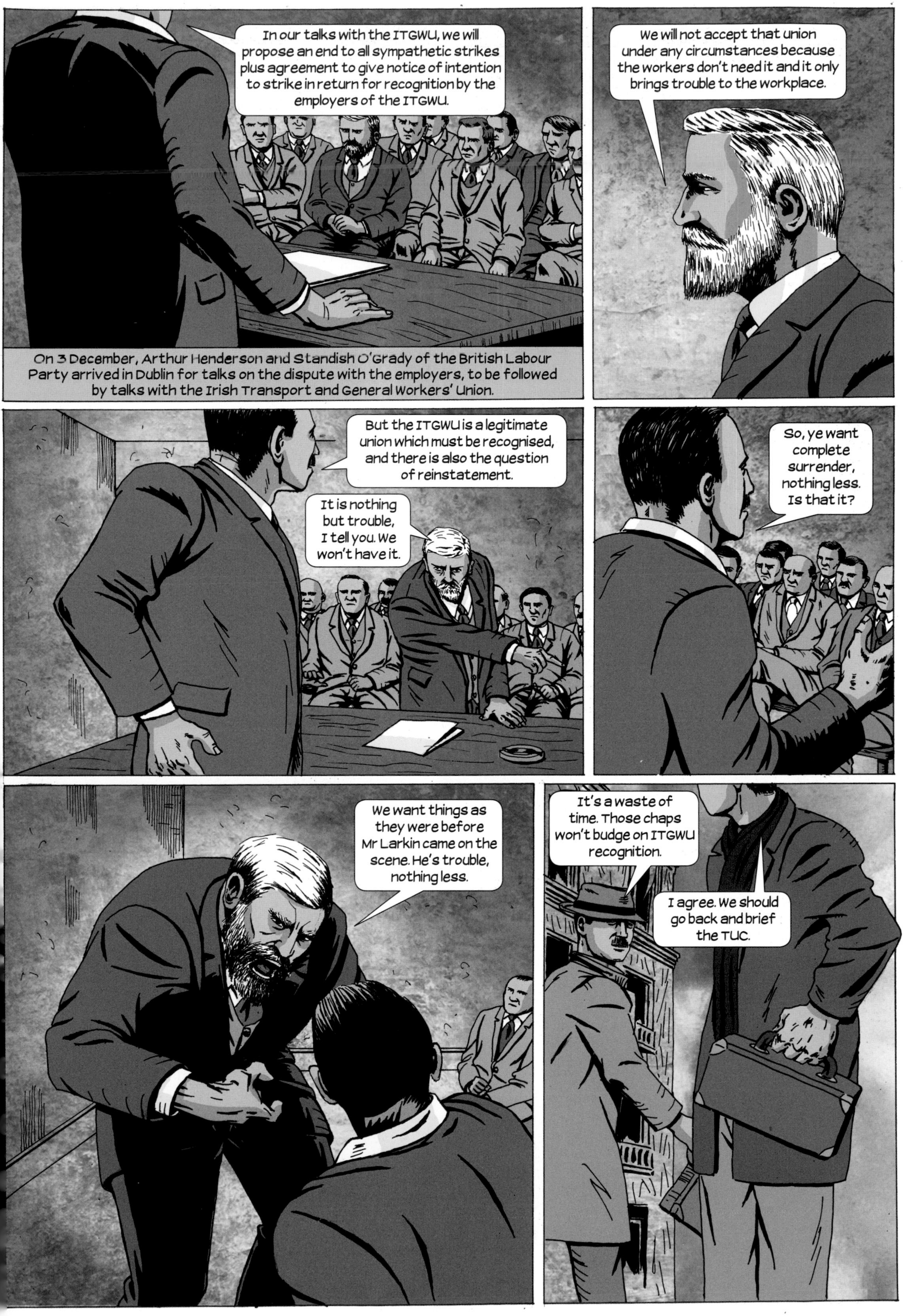
In our talks with the ITGWU, we will propose an end to all sympathetic strikes plus agreement to give notice of intention to strike in return for recognition by the employers of the ITGWU.
On 3 December, Arthur Henderson and Standish O'Grady of the British Labour Party arrived in Dublin for talks on the dispute with the employers, to be followed by talks with the Irish Transport and General Workers' Union.
We will not accept that union under any circumstances because the workers don't need it and it only brings trouble to the workplace.
But the ITGWU is a legitimate union which must be recognised, and there is also the question of reinstatement.
It is nothing but trouble, I tell you. We won't have it.
So, ye want complete surrender, nothing less. Is that it?
We want things as they were before Mr Larkin came on the scene. He's trouble, nothing less.
It's a waste of time. Those chaps won't budge on ITGWU recognition.
I agree. We should go back and brief the TUC.

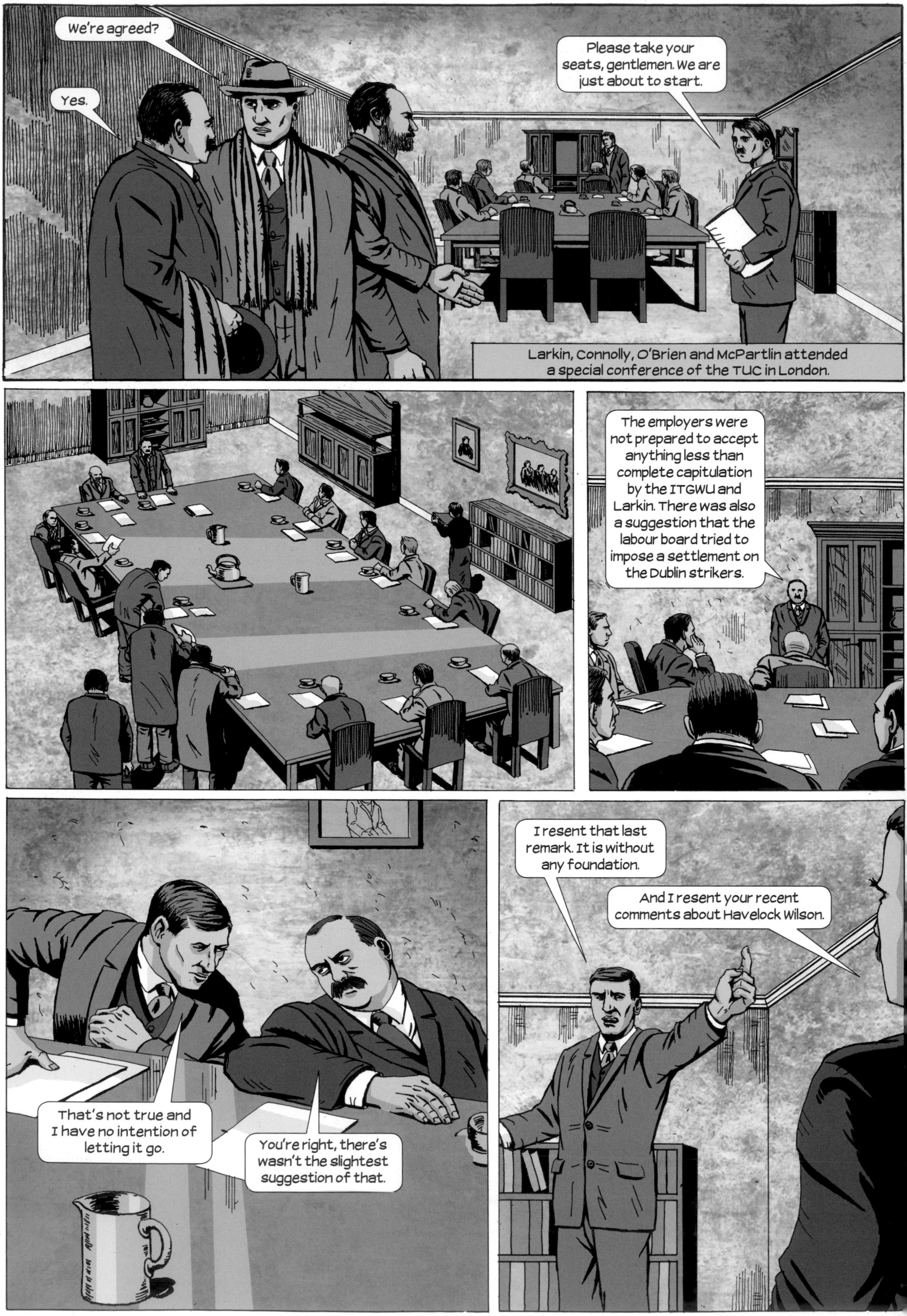

We're agreed?
Yes.
Please take your seats, gentlemen. We are just about to start.
Larkin, Connolly, O'Brien and McPartlin attended a special conference of the TUC in London.
The employers were not prepared to accept anything less than complete capitulation by the ITGWU and Larkin. There was also a suggestion that the labour board tried to impose a settlement on the Dublin strikers.
That's not true and I have no intention of letting it go.
You're right, there's wasn't the slightest suggestion of that.
I resent that last remark. It is without any foundation.
And I resent your recent comments about Havelock Wilson.

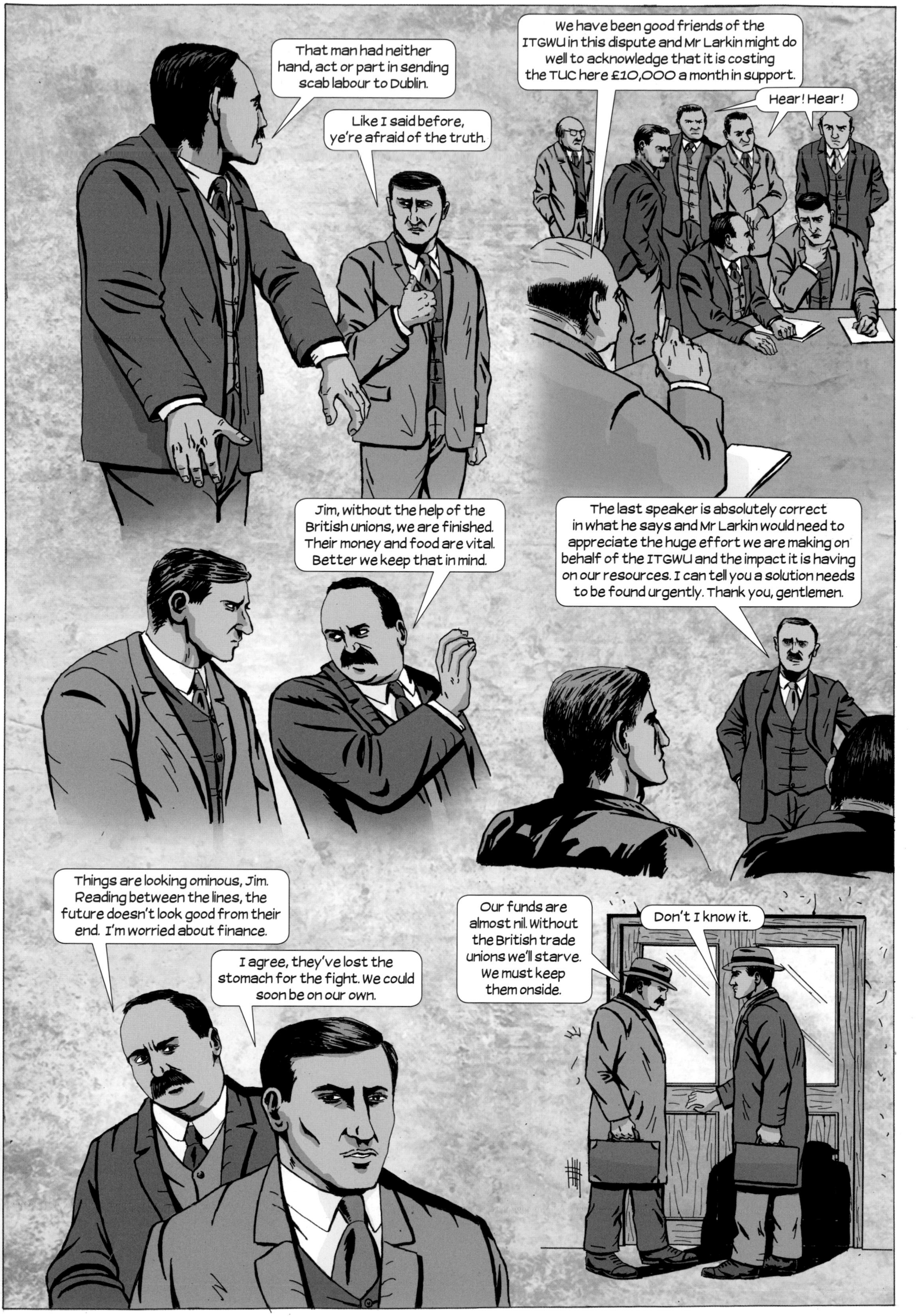
That man had neither hand, act or part in sending scab labour to Dublin.
Like I said before, ye're afraid of the truth.
We have been good friends of the ITGWU in this dispute and Mr Larkin might do well to acknowledge that it is costing the TUC here £10,000 a month in support.
Hear! Hear!
Jim, without the help of the British unions, we are finished. Their money and food are vital. Better we keep that in mind.
The last speaker is absolutely correct in what he says and Mr Larkin would need to appreciate the huge effort we are making on behalf of the ITGWU and the impact it is having on our resources. I can tell you a solution needs to be found urgently. Thank you, gentlemen.
Things are looking ominous, Jim. Reading between the lines, the future doesn't look good from their end. I'm worried about finance.
I agree, they've lost the stomach for the fight. We could soon be on our own.
Our funds are almost nil. Without the British trade unions we'll starve. We must keep them onside.
Don't I know it.

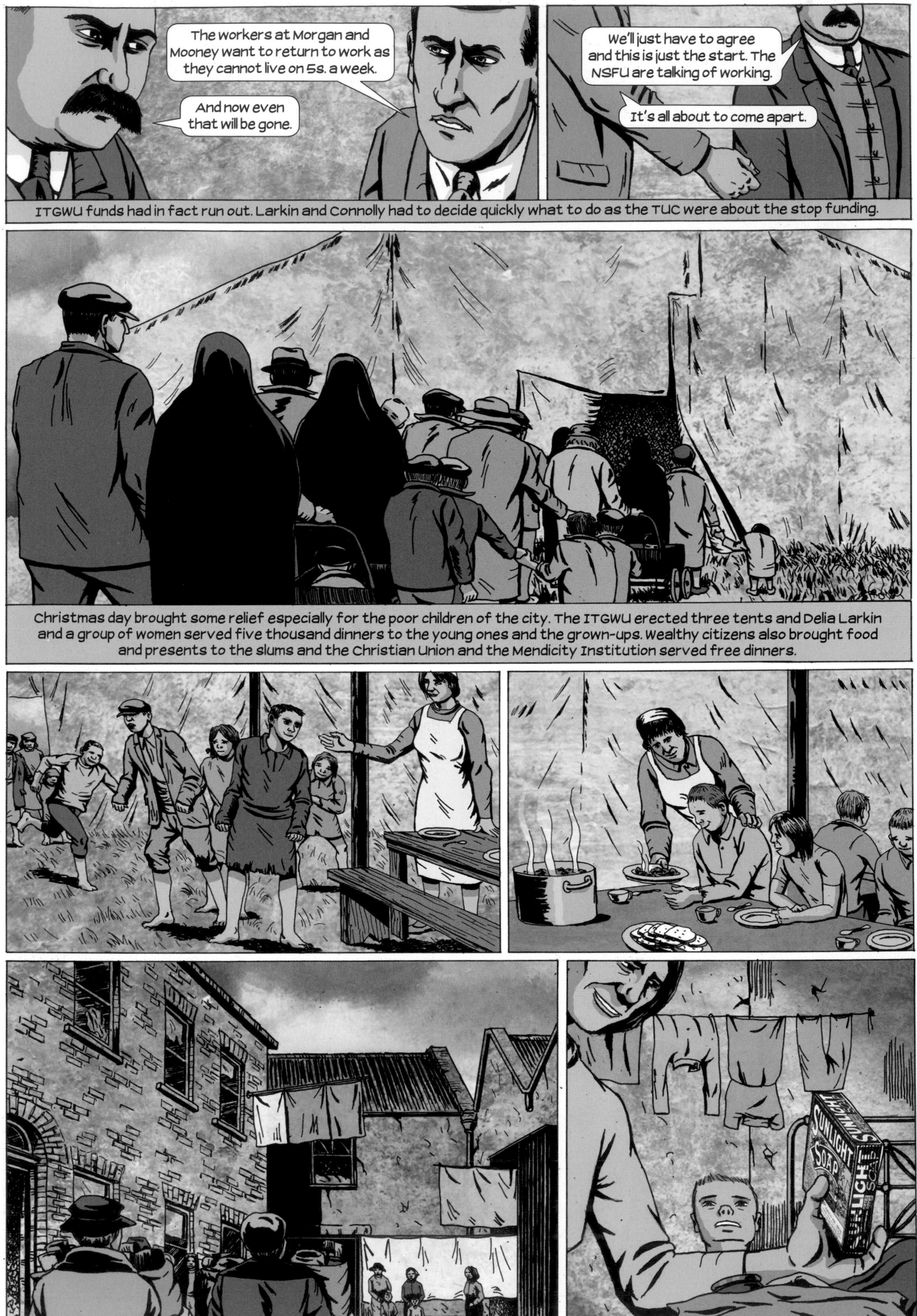
The workers at Morgan and Mooney want to return to work as they cannot live on 5s. a week.
And now even that will be gone.
We'll just have to agree and this is just the start. The NSFU are talking of working.
It's all about to come apart.
ITGWU funds had in fact run out. Larkin and Connolly had to decide quickly what to do as the TUC were about the stop funding.
Christmas day brought some relief especially for the poor children of the city. The ITGWU erected three tents and Delia Larkin and a group of women served five thousand dinners to the young ones and the grown-ups. Wealthy citizens also brought food and presents to the slums and the Christian Union and the Mendicity Institution served free dinners.
SUNLIGHT SOAP

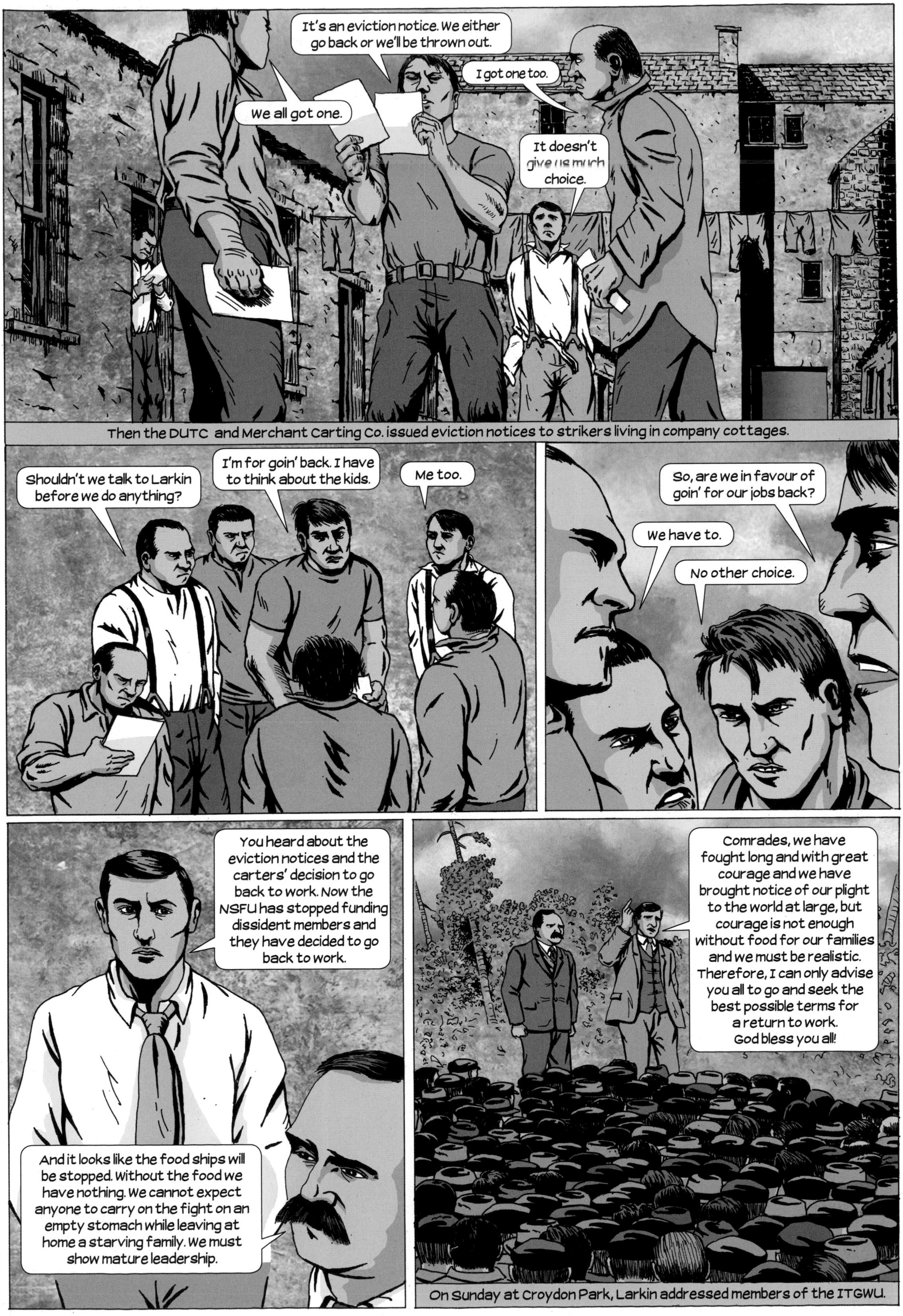
It's an eviction notice. We either go back or we'll be thrown out.
I got one too.
We all got one.
It doesn't give us much choice.
Then the DUTC and Merchant Carting Co. issued eviction notices to strikers living in company cottages.
Shouldn't we talk to Larkin before we do anything?
I'm for goin' back. I have to think about the kids.
Me too.
So, are we in favour of goin' for our jobs back?
We have to.
No other choice.
You heard about the eviction notices and the carters' decision to go back to work. Now the NSFU has stopped funding dissident members and they have decided to go back to work.
And it looks like the food ships will be stopped. Without the food we have nothing. We cannot expect anyone to carry on the fight on an empty stomach while leaving at home a starving family. We must show mature leadership.
Comrades, we have fought long and with great courage and we have brought notice of our plight to the world at large, but courage is not enough without food for our families and we must be realistic. Therefore, I can only advise you all to go and seek the best possible terms for a return to work. God bless you all!
On Sunday at Croydon Park, Larkin addressed members of the ITGWU.

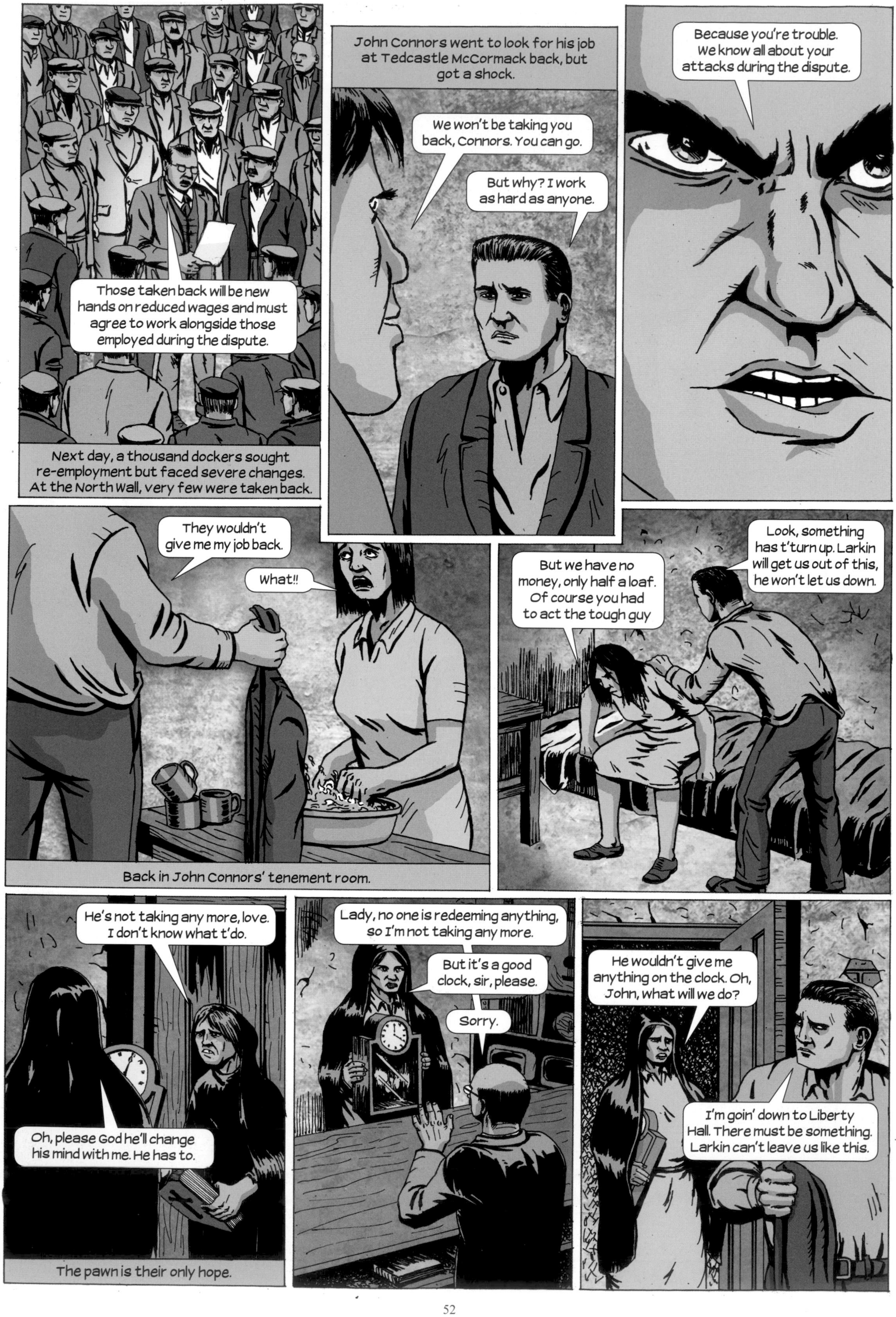
Those taken back will be new hands on reduced wages and must agree to work alongside those employed during the dispute.
Next day, a thousand dockers sought re-employment but faced severe changes. At the North Wall, very few were taken back.
John Connors went to look for his job at Tedcastle McCormack back, but got a shock.
We won't be taking you back, Connors. You can go.
But why? I work as hard as anyone.
Because you're trouble. We know all about your attacks during the dispute.
They wouldn't give me my job back.
What!!
Back in John Connors' tenement room.
But we have no money, only half a loaf. Of course you had to act the tough guy
Look, something has t'turn up. Larkin will get us out of this, he won't let us down.
He's not taking any more, love. I don't know what t'do.
Oh, please God he'll change his mind with me. He has to.
The pawn is their only hope.
Lady, no one is redeeming anything, so I'm not taking any more.
But it's a good clock, sir, please.
Sorry.
He wouldn't give me anything on the clock. Oh, John, what will we do?
I'm goin' down to Liberty Hall. There must be something. Larkin can't leave us like this.

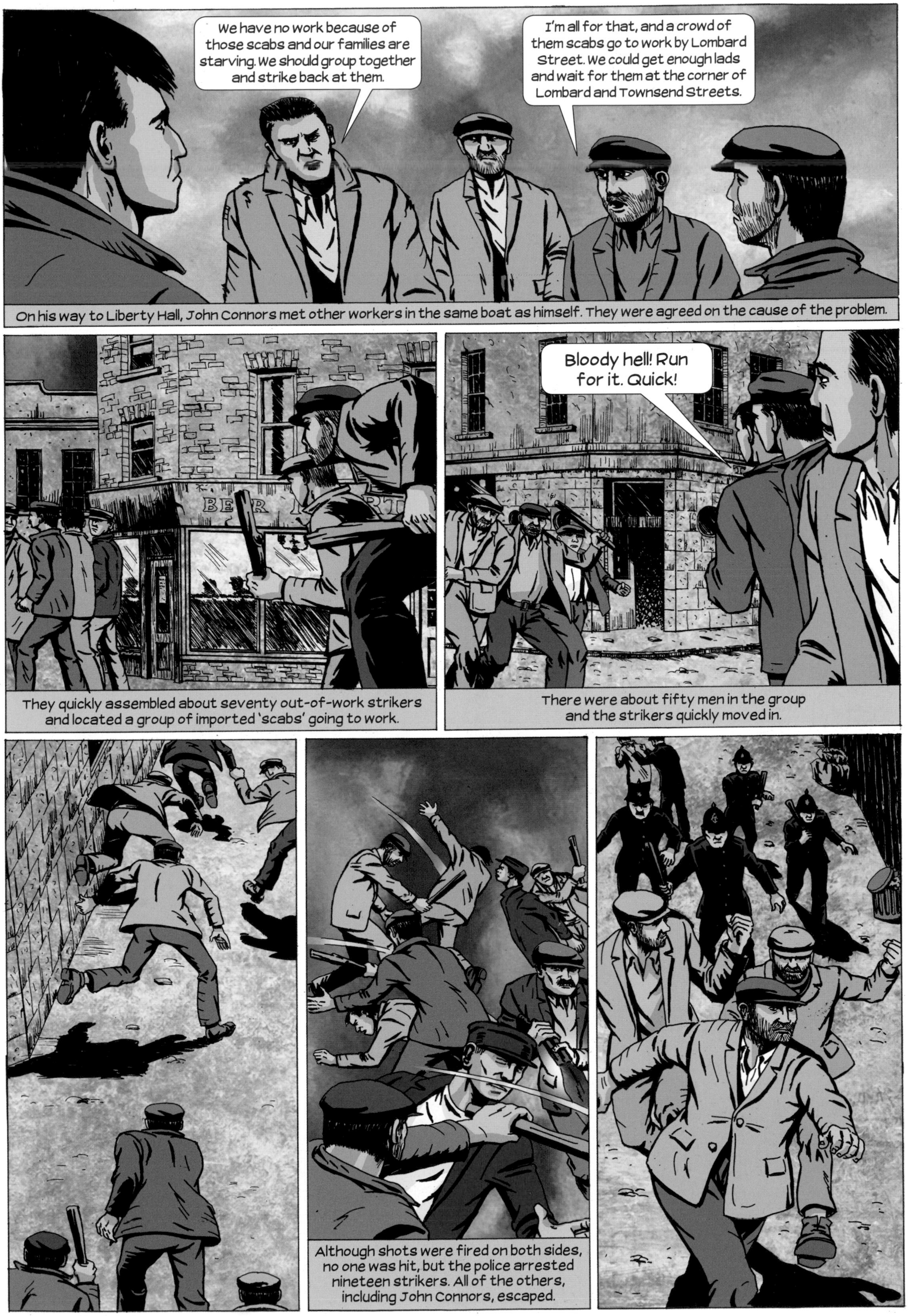
We have no work because of those scabs and our families are starving. We should group together and strike back at them.
I'm all for that, and a crowd of them scabs go to work by Lombard Street. We could get enough lads and wait for them at the corner of Lombard and Townsend Streets.
On his way to Liberty Hall, John Connors met other workers in the same boat as himself. They were agreed on the cause of the problem.
They quickly assembled about seventy out-of-work strikers and located a group of imported 'scabs' going to work.
Bloody hell! Run for it. Quick!
There were about fifty men in the group and the strikers quickly moved in.
Although shots were fired on both sides, no one was hit, but the police arrested nineteen strikers. All of the others, including John Connors, escaped.

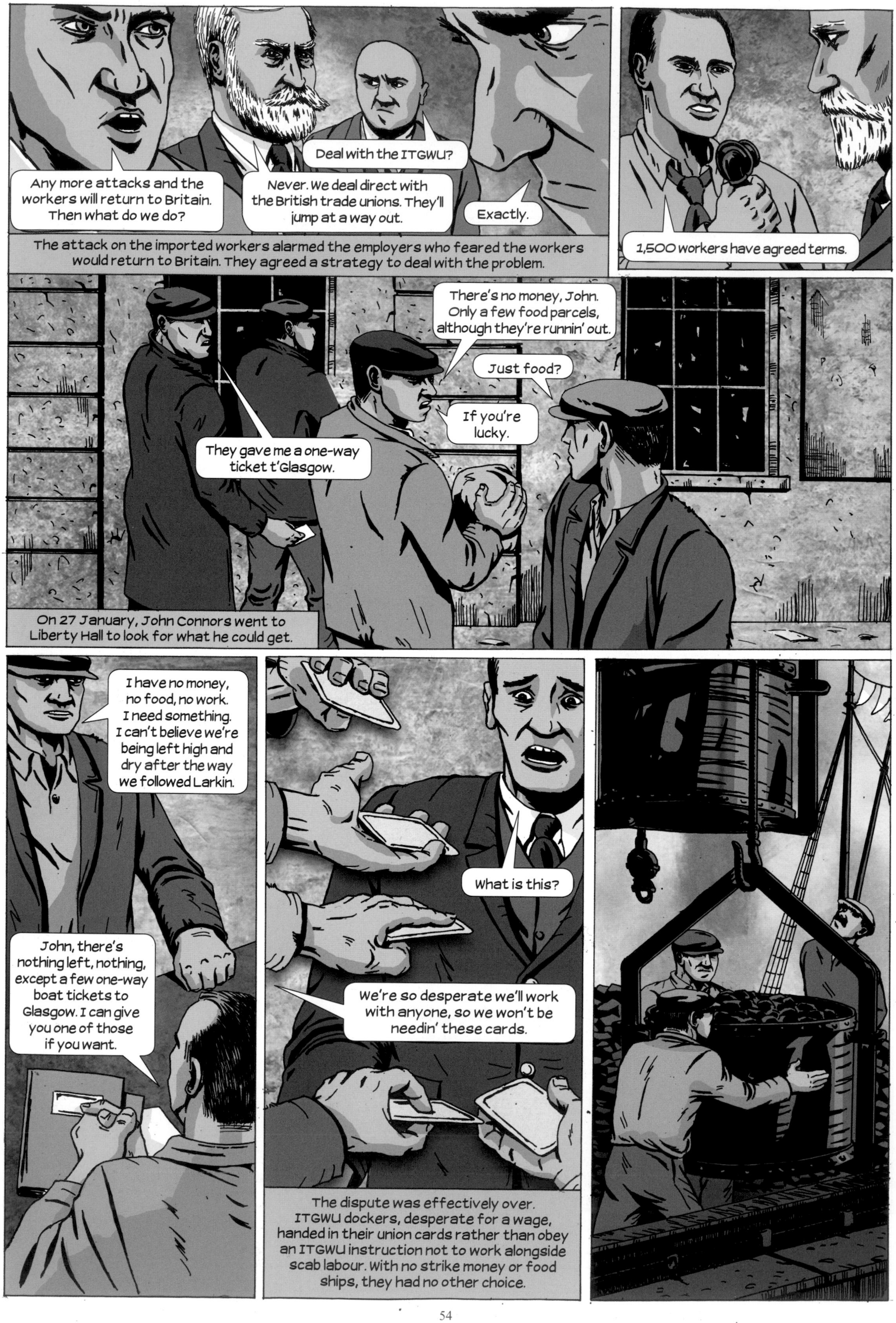
Any more attacks and the workers will return to Britain. Then what do we do?
Never. We deal direct with the British trade unions. They'll jump at a way out.
Deal with the ITGWU?
Exactly.
The attack on the imported workers alarmed the employers who feared the workers would return to Britain. They agreed a strategy to deal with the problem.
1,500 workers have agreed terms.
On 27 January, John Connors went to Liberty Hall to look for what he could get.
There's no money, John. Only a few food parcels, although they're runnin' out.
Just food?
If you're lucky.
They gave me a one-way ticket t'Glasgow.
I have no money, no food, no work. I need something. I can't believe we're being left high and dry after the way we followed Larkin.
John, there's nothing left, nothing, except a few one-way boat tickets to Glasgow. I can give you one of those if you want.
What is this?
We're so desperate we'll work with anyone, so we won't be needin' these cards.
The dispute was effectively over. ITGWU dockers, desperate for a wage, handed in their union cards rather than obey an ITGWU instruction not to work alongside scab labour. With no strike money or food ships, they had no other choice.

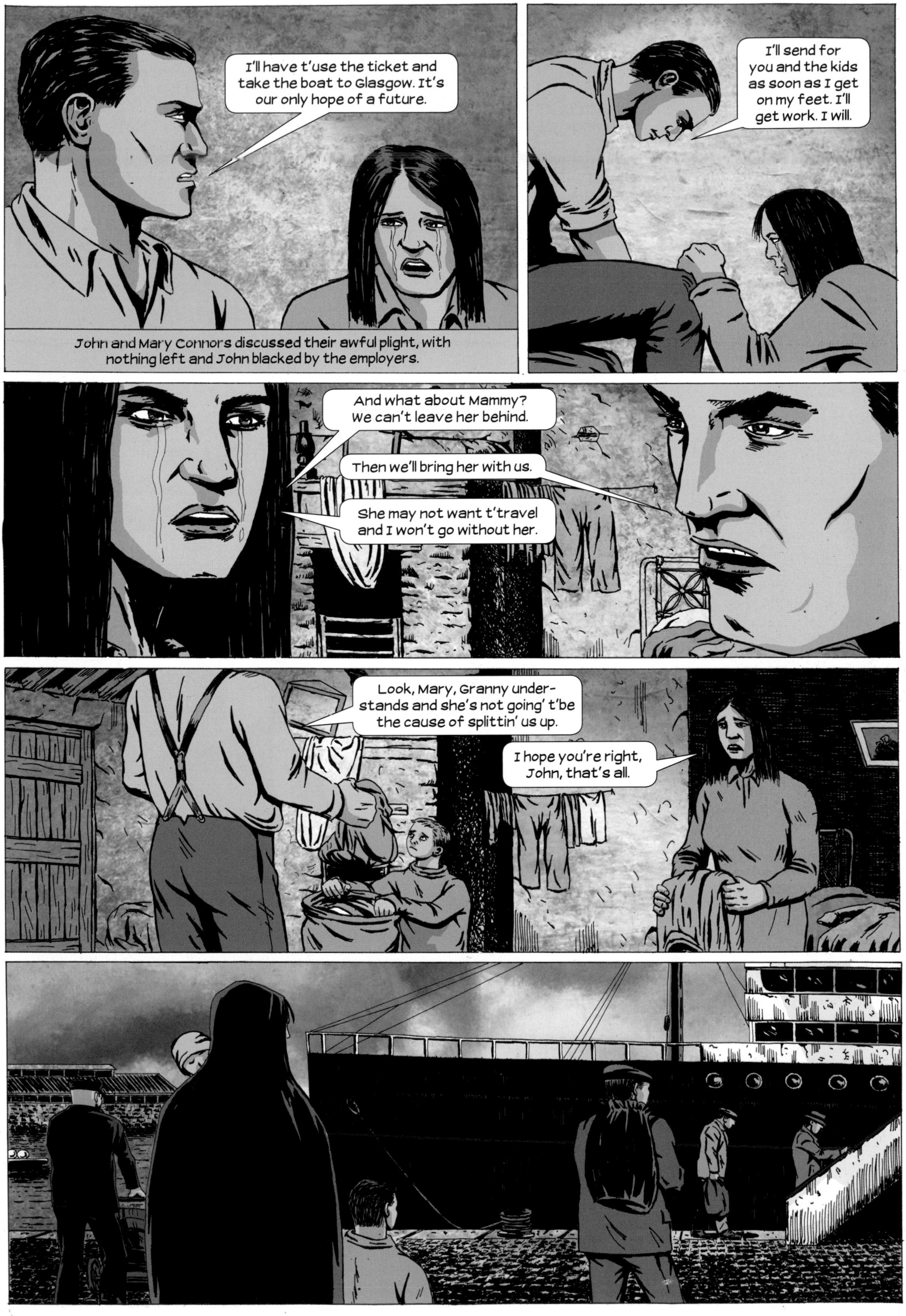
I'll have t'use the ticket and take the boat to Glasgow. It's our only hope of a future.
John and Mary Connors discussed their awful plight, with nothing left and John blacked by the employers.
I'll send for you and the kids as soon as I get on my feet. I'll get work. I will.
And what about Mammy? We can't leave her behind.
Then we'll bring her with us.
She may not want t'travel and I won't go without her.
Look, Mary, Granny under-stands and she's not going' t'be the cause of splittin' us up.
I hope you're right, John, that's all.

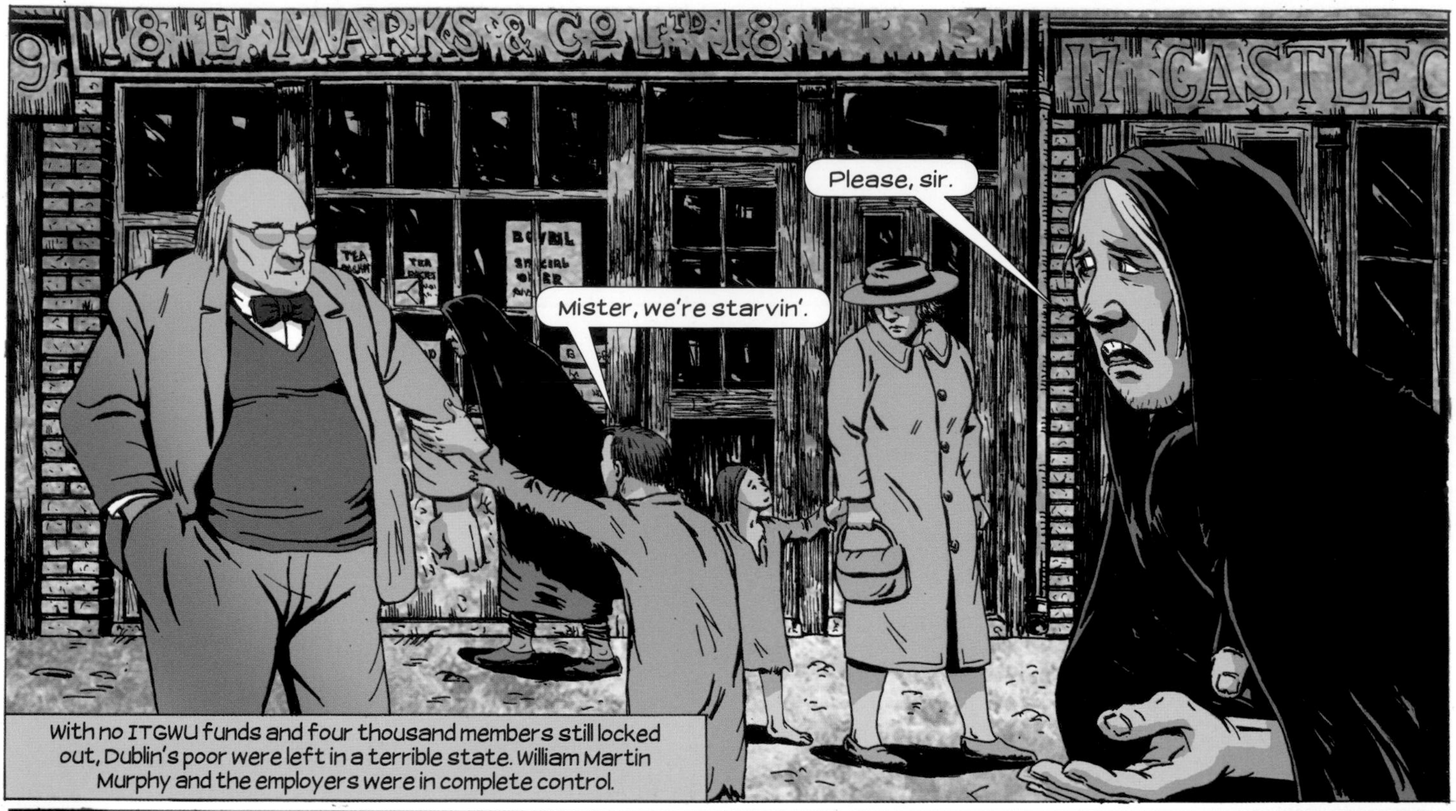
18 E. MARKS & Co. Ltd 18
17 CASTLEC
Please, sir.
Mister, we're starvin'.
With no ITGWU funds and four thousand members still locked out, Dublin's poor were left in a terrible state. William Martin Murphy and the employers were in complete control.

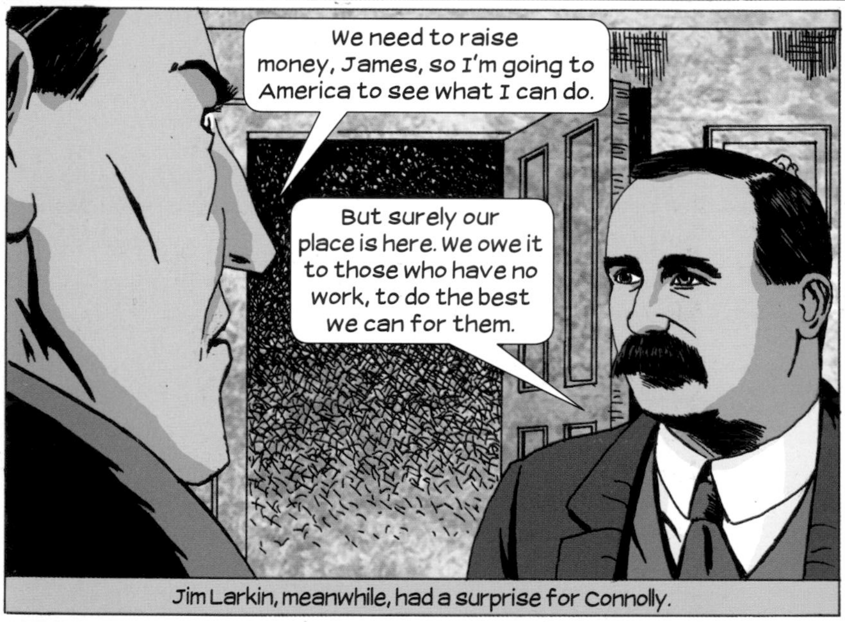
We need to raise money, James, so I'm going to America to see what I can do.
But surely our place is here. We owe it to those who have no work, to do the best we can for them.
Jim Larkin, meanwhile, had a surprise for Connolly.

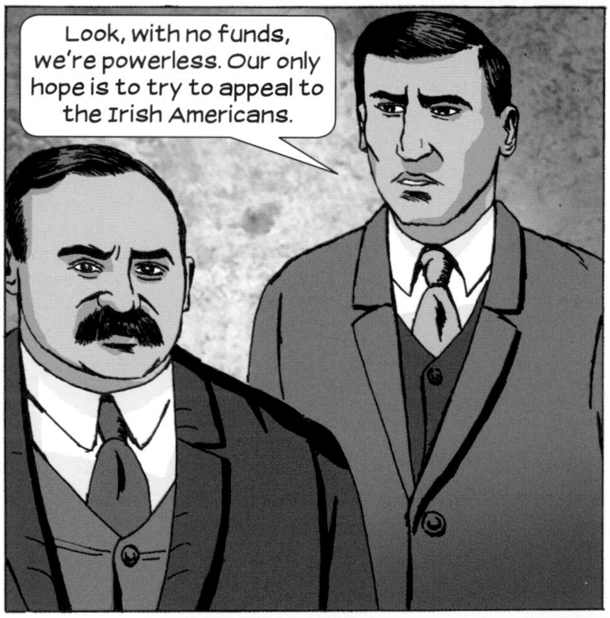
Look, with no funds, we're powerless. Our only hope is to try to appeal to the Irish Americans.

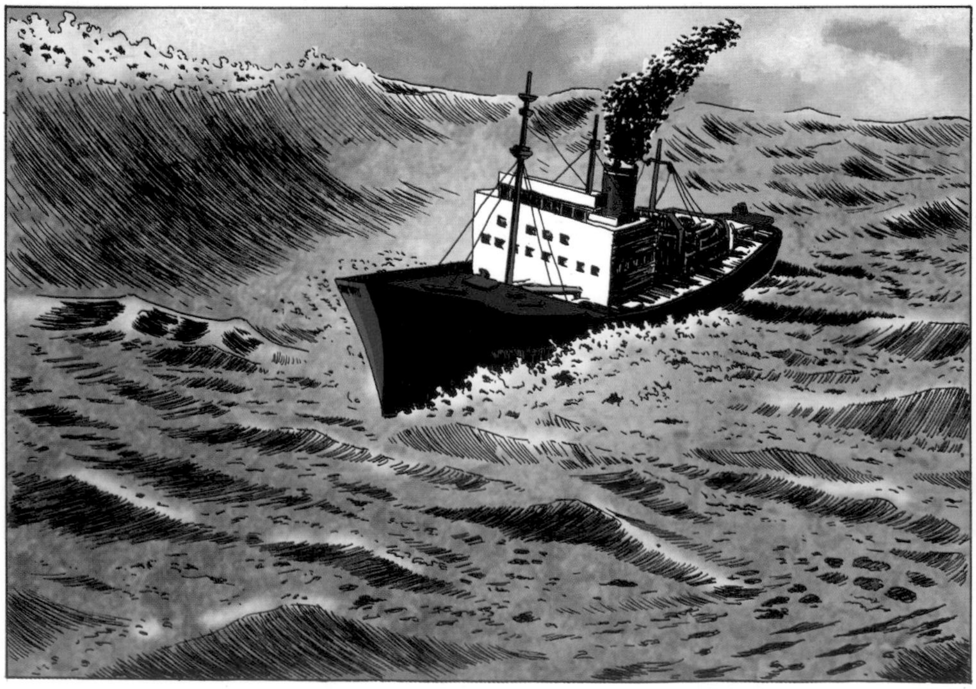

Larkin went to America in October 1914; Connolly became General Secretary of the ITGWU. He rallied the remnants of the union and used the circumstances caused by the war to compel the employers to improve wages and conditions.

His execution in 1916 provoked a huge increase in union support around the country and in 1919 there were 102,823 members in 433 branches.

William O'Brien took over as General Secretary on his release from jail in 1919. Larkin, on his return in April 1923, was not prepared to work with the union executive and was expelled on 14 March 1924. He then formed The Workers Union of Ireland.

In 1990 the two unions amalgamated to form SIPTU, which is now the largest union in the country and based in Liberty Hall.

HISTORICAL NOTE

The 1913 Lockout, or Larkin's Labour War, was the most significant and influential labour dispute in Irish history.

Living conditions for Dublin's poor in 1913 were atrocious, with thousands of families crammed into crumbling, disease-ridden tenements. Before 'Big Jim' Larkin set up the Irish Transport and General Workers' Union (ITGWU) in 1909, there was no union for unskilled workers, so they were at the mercy of their employers and had no way to lobby for better pay and conditions, but by 1913 the ITGWU had a membership of 10,000 and was becoming a force to be reckoned with, to the chagrin of many employers. The efforts of employers and business owners, led by William Martin Murphy, to remove the ITGWU from the equation led to the Lockout, and to five months of upheaval, suffering and privation in Dublin City.

Though the unions didn't 'win' – the workers, some of whom were near starvation, returned to work in early 1914, with many of them required to pledge not to join a union – the Lockout marked a major turning point in labour relations; business in the capital and beyond was severely damaged, and employers never tried to break a union in the same way.

The 1913 Lockout also marked the beginning of a turbulent decade in Irish history, from 1913 to 1922. The Lockout brought James Connolly, among others, to prominence; Connolly was a co-founder of the Irish Citizen Army and went on to become one of the prime movers in the 1916 Rising, which led to the War of Independence, the Civil War, and eventually, the establishment of the Irish Free State, precursor to the Irish Republic, in December 1922.

ALSO FROM
GERRY HUNT

O'BRIEN
BLOOD UPON THE ROSE
EASTER 1916
THE REBELLION THAT SET IRELAND FREE
GERRY HUNT

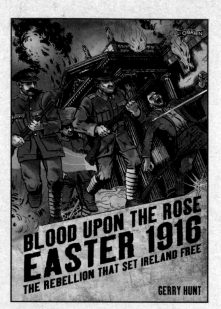

Blood Upon The Rose
Easter 1916: The Rebellion That Set Ireland Free

The rebellion that set Ireland free, told as a graphic novel.

The 1916 Easter Rising was an attempt by a small group of militant Irish republicans to win independence from Britain. It was the most significant rebellion in Ireland. Though a military failure, it set Ireland on the road to freedom from Britain.

The book covers the story from the early planning to the final executions and includes the tragic romance between Joseph Plunkett and Grace Gifford.

Following on from the success of political graphic novels such as Maus and Persepolis, this is accessible, informative and insightful history at its best.

At War with the Empire
Ireland's Fight for Independence

O'BRIEN
AT WAR WITH THE EMPIRE
IRELAND'S FIGHT FOR INDEPENDENCE
GERRY HUNT

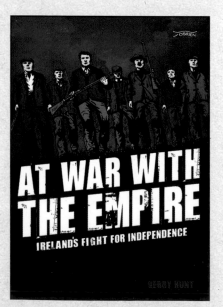

The Easter Rising of 1916, with its Proclamation of Independence, lit the spark that would eventually blaze into a full-scale War of Independence in Ireland.

Though the 1916 Rising was put down within a week, the harshness of the British response greatly increased support for Sinn Fein, the Republican party. By 1918 disaffectation with British rule was widespread. When Sinn Féin won a majority of seats in the 1918 election they vowed to set up their own Irish parliament. The first Irish parliament, the Dáil, was formed on 21 January 1919. It reaffirmed the 1916 proclamation with the Declaration of Independence, and issued a 'Message to the Free Nations of the World' that stated that there was 'an existing state of war between Ireland and England'. On that same day, the first shots were fired in the Irish War of Independence.

This is the story of that war.